BLACK AND MAINSTREAM PRESS' FRAMING OF RACIAL PROFILING

A Historical Perspective

Mia Nodeen Moody, Ph.D.

University Press of America,® Inc.
Lanham · Boulder · New York · Toronto · Plymouth, UK

Copyright © 2008 by
University Press of America®, Inc.
4501 Forbes Boulevard
Suite 200
Lanham, Maryland 20706
UPA Acquisitions Department (301) 459-3366

Estover Road
Plymouth PL6 7PY
United Kingdom

Library of Congress Control Number: 2008921687
ISBN-13: 978-0-7618-4036-7 (paperback : alk. paper)
ISBN-10: 0-7618-4036-2 (paperback : alk. paper)

Dedication

I wish to dedicate this book to my family, particularly my children—Heidi, Timothy and William. Thank you all for enduring the many hours I spent finishing this project.

Table of Contents

List of Tables

Foreword

In those tense days following the Sept. 11, 2001, attack on the United States, airport security at the time included what was called "random" searches of passengers boarding an airplane. In other words, not everyone was searched—only passengers selected according to a randomization scheme.

When the 9/11 tragedy occurred that fall semester, I was a visiting professor at the University of Texas School of Journalism teaching a news writing class. A student's story assignment about airport security quickly revealed that 9/11 was a milestone event for the issue of racial profiling in general and racial profiling of Middle Easterners in particular.

I will never forget the lead. It was funny, yet profound.

In that lead, the source, who was of Middle Eastern descent, laughed when she sarcastically said that she was "randomly searched" every time she boarded an airplane.

Even though U.S. society, on the whole, was already prone to make snap, often incorrect stereotypical judgments about people who didn't look or act like them, 9/11, no doubt, escalated society's fear of and racial profiling of Middle Easterners.

Racial profiling is not a new concept to U.S. society. It has a controversial past in the United States. Blacks have suffered through this phenomenon since the days of captivity. And more recently, charges of racial profiling of minorities (mostly African American and Hispanic) dominated many news reports of the 1990s. The decade before that, the federal government's "War on Drugs" relied heavily on racial profiling to identify drug dealers and users. Some would even argue that the "War on Drugs" was fueled as much by economic factors relating to the 1980s recession as by "White Backlash" politics of the "Law and Order" era of the 1970s. This was the period when many whites reacted negatively to the civil rights gains by blacks and urban disturbances of the 1960s and the affirmative action programs of the 1970s. Too many politicians preyed on the fears of whites with promises of bringing law and order to cities plagued with violence and limiting entitlement programs for people seeking something for nothing. Predominantly, the faces on these issues, according to the mainstream media, were black.

During this period, too many media images of African Americans were of angry, malcontented people who were violent, wanted handouts and spent too much time being cool. These negative stereotypical images lessened the impact of any complaints by blacks of such charges as racial profiling and police brutality. As a result, many mainstream media took a more cautious view than did African-American media of these racially tinged issues, thereby mitigating the negative impact on the police. "After all, the police are just doing their jobs" to control rioting and drugs, much mainstream media coverage implied. African-American media, more often than not, had an opposite view.

Given this backdrop of social, economic and political issues of the last four decades, those of us who study communication know that the final news product is the result of a complex set of factors—many of which Mia Moody addresses in this book with analyses of news reports about racial profiling. In terms of newspaper coverage, historically, for African Americans, these factors certainly helped to produce more negative than positive stories in the mainstream media.

The argument that Moody makes is that the salience of such emotional issues as racial profiling depends greatly on who is reporting what to whom through what channel. Who is reporting makes a big difference in what is reported and how it is reported. That point was made clear in this book, a comparative study of selected issues relating to racial profiling and its treatment in black and mainstream newspapers.

To prove her point, Moody devises a simple, yet elegant, research design that compares news reports on racial profiling in black and mainstream newspapers in an analysis that combines concepts of framing and gatekeeping. She does this by conducting a content and textual analysis of articles on racial profiling in black and mainstream newspapers published three years before and three years after 9/11.

Because black and mainstream media report for dissimilar social groups with often opposing ideological goals, their coverage of issues is frequently divergent, essentially different. Time and again, black and mainstream newspapers have been ideological opposites. The present study asks the question: Can this common enemy that brought us the 9/11 tragedy bring these two media opposites together in their perspectives on the issue of racial profiling?

This is an important question since the origin and continued existence of black newspapers and black media in general are the result of mainstream media's lack of and/or distorted coverage of African Americans. Just like these two media types have taken opposite sides on many issues in the 180 years since the first black newspaper was founded, they did the same with the issue of racial profiling before 9/11. The founding in 1827 of "Freedom's Journal," the first black newspaper, was prompted by the refusal of the "New York Sun" editor to honor a request by African-American leaders for the newspaper to retract a derogatory article about blacks. It was common for newspapers at that time to publish negative articles that painted stereotypical images of the city's black population. With "Freedom's Journal," the die for African-America newspapers was cast: Black-controlled content was needed to counter that of the predominant white media. "We wish to plead our own case," the editors of that first black newspaper boldly told the world.

That they did. Then, as now, the black press often told different stories from their white-controlled counterparts.

Stories today about racial profiling are told no differently. There are at least two sides—sometimes more, depending on the political context. Through the years, racial profiling has been framed on one side as a social injustice and on the other as a useful police tactic. Because reporters use their own cultural/political perspectives to decide what news is and what news is not, they, as creators of the message, therefore, create the frames for stories. How will the story be told? In turn, the editors, also with their unique cultural perspectives, decide what information gets out of the news gate. Will the story be told?

So when we juxtapose the historical relationship of police/authorities and the African-American community, given the social context, it is predictable how the news framers and gatekeepers are going to package the information in their newspapers for their constituent readers. Of course, they do it with sources they choose. These can be sources they are familiar with, sources who support their point of view, sources who oppose their point of view and many other categories of sources. How they choose their sources is an important question. Whom will they talk to to tell the story to their constituent readers? The police/authorities who more than likely initiated the story with some kind of official action? The victims themselves? The community activists who organized meetings and protests to complain about the official actions? The elected officials who are charged with making laws that can affect official police policies and actions? Citizens and other community experts who may have opinions on the actions?

Moody's study answers these critical questions and more about what sources will be included to tell the story. These sources help to create the content of the story about racial profiling. Now, the big question in framing literature that W.A. Gamson raises and that Moody addresses in this study is this: "What is the basic source of controversy or concern in this issue?"

The answer to this question sets the stage for a debate between competing media, in this case black newspapers versus mainstream newspapers, about claims and counterclaims in what becomes a battle between community elites for control of the message. This is where the elites of different social groups join in what is essentially a civic or community discussion.

This civic discussion seeks to answer Gamson's question, which is a classic quest for meaning. Who is saying what to whom with what effect with what meaning?

Given this, in studying meaning, this book examines both literal content (what is written) and structural presentation elements. The following types of literal content were examined: portrayal of different groups, use of catchphrases and uses of frames. Structural presentation elements studied were story placement, use of sources, types of editorial content and uses of frames. As stated earlier, all of these components (literal content and structural presentation elements) come together to create meaning.

Five research questions were posed to address the impact of the above content elements. The findings are briefly listed below. There was:

- No significant difference in placement of stories. Before 9/11, most stories about racial profiling in both black and mainstream newspapers appeared inside the newspapers as opposed to the front page.
- Significant difference in the types of stories on racial profiling. Both black and mainstream newspapers ran a higher percentage of straight-news stories than editorials. Post 9/11, it was the other way around.
- Significant difference in the use of locally bylined stories versus the use of wire stories. For both black and mainstream newspapers, pre-9/11, most of the articles in both media were locally produced. After 9/11, wire stories increased in black publications, while the number decreased in mainstream media.

Preface: Racial Profiling an Evolving Epidemic?

I remember being a little surprised when police officers pulled me over while I was moving out of an apartment and into a house after graduating from college. At the time—1991—racial profiling had not become a popular catchphrase. I thought maybe they were being vigilant, and I did not have second thoughts as they released me without an explanation for pulling me over. However, as I became older and wiser, I began to understand why I had been stopped. I was a young, black woman driving around in a neighborhood with a car full of furniture. I must have stolen these items I'm sure they must have thought.

Today, times have changed. Most African Americans know all too well about racial profiling. Parents warn their children, especially their sons, about the importance of not appearing too sassy or aggressive around police officers. African American women know that if they are dressed too nicely or if they are slightly overweight, they will almost always be searched prior to flying on any airline.

Racial profiling and its influence on minorities has been a newsworthy topic since the late 1990s when front-page news stories and editorials in both the national and local press began to illustrate the individual and societal costs of racial profiling, or the discriminatory practice by police of treating skin color as an indication of possible criminality. September 11 added yet another dimension to the racial paradigm: Arabs, Muslims and other groups were added to the equation. Blacks breathed a sigh of relief as they disappeared from the radar screen—if only for a short period of time.

I remember the fear and sadness I felt the day the Twin Towers were obliterated and terrorism became public enemy No. 1 in the United States. I was sitting in class with about eight other students at the University of Texas. As a first-year doctoral student, I watched the immediate coverage, and the vulnerability of the United States was revealed for the first time in my life. We sat dumbfounded and somewhat betrayed as we watch the strong United States suffer at the hands of an enemy. Most of us had taken for granted the perception of a safe haven. But never again after that day. The September 11 attacks are among the most significant events in the United States to have occurred so far in the 21st century. The event had resounding economic, social, political, and military effects that included the expense and time incurred in repairing the damage done, as well as the lives that changed forever after witnessing the vulnerability of the United States. Racial profiling became a catchphrase often heard on nightly newscasts.

All of these variables led to my dissertation topic: Black and Mainstream Press' Framing of Racial Profiling Before and After September 11, which later led to this book. This study was warranted because history has shown that mainstream and black press outlets have different ideas or perceptions of what is important and what should be covered in their respective newspapers. The two have different missions and self-images that have arisen out of specific historical circumstances, often as a response to oppression or misrepresentation in the case of minority newspapers. The two have different missions and self-images that have arisen out of specific historical circumstances, often as a response to oppression or misrepresentation in the case of minority newspapers. Examples of instances where the two types of newspapers covered issues differently include: the Clarence Thomas confirmation hearings, the 1992 Los Angeles riots following the Rodney King verdict, and the O.J. Simpson murder trial (Dates and Barlow, 1993 and Martindale, 1990). Although instances of overt racism appear to be few, studies have shown that African-American and general press outlets handle stories differently.

These differences have been documented in many studies, but something that hasn't been documented is whether a tragedy can bring them closer together in their scope. One would speculate that the issue would have to be deeply entrenched in a community and there would have to be some type of tragedy that would produce a change that would allow the issue to be studied under a different environment.

September 11 produced a media climate that made both black and mainstream newspapers stand up and take note. One of the questions I pondered was whether communities act differently when injustice is served against two different groups against the backdrop of a dramatic event. Will black press and mainstream media become more similar when faced with a common enemy, i.e., terrorists? Hence, the study also examined how mainstream and black press newspapers framed the phenomena of "racial profiling" three years before and three years after the September 11 terrorist attacks. It looked particularly at frames, ethnic groups, source selection and article emphasis. Results indicate that even in the face of a tragedy, black press reporters did not waiver in their position and continued to cover issues from a "black perspective." On the other hand, mainstream newspapers altered their coverage during the high-stress period and began to portray racial profiling as an anti-Arab/terrorist tactic that is acceptable in some cases. This study helps answer the question of whether black press newspapers are necessary in today's society. The answer is a resounding yes. They still carry a unique viewpoint. Until the gap that divides African American and other readers ceases to exist, the black press will remain an important staple in the black community.

Mia Moody, Ph.D.
Waco, TX 76798
July, 2007

Acknowledgements

First, I wish to thank my adviser, Dr. Stephen Reese, for all of his help and guidance throughout my studies at the University of Texas, as well as with my dissertation. I also wish to thank my committee members: Professor Rosental Alves, Dr. Maggie Rivas Rodriguez, Dr. Charles Whitney and Dr. Karin Wilkins. Your advice and kind words throughout this project motivated as well as inspired me in ways that I could not imagine. Next, I wish to acknowledge my Baylor University family, particularly students Kelly Coleman, Jennifer Simmons and Andrew Ortiz, for help with coding and proofreading. I would also like to thank the Baylor Statistics Department for its guidance in helping me choose the proper statistical methods for my study. I also wish to acknowledge colleagues Reginald Owens and Dawnica Jackson for their input in helping me develop the final draft and forward for the book. Finally, I wish to thank my parents, Jerry and Nelda Moody, for their many years of encouragement and guidance. Most notably, my mother for the hours she spent proofreading this document. Without all of you, the completion of this major task would not have been possible.

Chapter One: Introduction

The September 11 terrorist attacks are undoubtedly the most significant incidents to have occurred in the United States so far in the 21st century. Citizens living in the United States endured changes in their lives both physically and mentally, economically and spiritually after witnessing the vulnerability of their country at the hands of terrorists. Of particular interest is the effect the tragedy had on the media's coverage and knowledge of racial profiling. Until the late 1990s, racial profiling was a buzzword that people often heard in passing but were not quite sure of its definition. However, after the September 11 terrorist attacks, the term became a household catchphrase discussed daily on many newscasts.

Journalists generally used the expression to describe the practice of stopping and inspecting people passing through public places where the reason for the stop was a statistical profile of the detainee's race or ethnicity (Kinsley, 2001). Post-September 11, the focal point shifted from cars to airplanes and from African Americans to Arabs or people with ancestries originating from areas of the world categorized as Arab (De la Cruz & Brittingham, 2003). To illustrate this shift in trends, the already popular catchphrase, "Driving While Black," mutated and journalists added to their vocabularies, "Flying While Arab" or "Driving While Brown," alluding to the fact that law enforcers singled out this latest target for no apparent reason other than skin color and/or attire. Over the next few months following the attack, "racial profiling" became a catchall phrase for many types of profiling including religious, ethnic, and racial.

Today, the definitions for racial profiling are more encompassing. For example, the U.S. Department of Justice Resources Guide on Racial Profiling defines it as, "Any police-initiated action that relies on race, ethnicity, or national origin rather than the behavior of an individual or information that leads police officers to a particular individual who has been identified as being, or having been, engaged in criminal activity." Amnesty International USA adds to the definition the idea that members of certain groups and religions are often targets. It defines racial profiling as: "The targeting of individuals and groups by law enforcement officials, even partially, on the basis of race, ethnicity, national origin, or religion, except where there is trustworthy information, relevant to the locality and a timeframe that links persons belonging to one of the aforementioned groups to an identified criminal incident or scheme" (Kasravi, 2004).

Before September 11, some articles depicted racial profiling as a social injustice, while others portrayed it as smart tactic. For instance, Derbyshire (2001) defended the practice as a sensible law enforcement technique during which police officers employ the laws of probability to make the best use of their scarce resources in attacking crime. Similarly, Callahan (2001) wrote that the police engage in racial profiling for simple efficiency: "A policeman who concentrates a disproportionate amount of his limited time and resources on young black men is going to uncover far more crimes, and therefore be far more successful in his career, than one who biases his attention toward, say, middle-aged Asian women" (p. 1).

After September 11, the general population and the media showed signs of a transformation in beliefs regarding the issue of racial profiling. The horrendous nature of the tragedy and journalists' addition of victims based on religious affiliation or ethnicity to their coverage presented an interesting dichotomy. On one hand, reporters worried about a victim's civil and privacy rights. On the other hand, they questioned protecting one's self from the diverse groups under investigation. For example, an August 17, 2004, USA Today article by Michelle Malkin stated that racial profiling based on race, religion, or nationality, is justified when the United States' national security is on the line. She added that targeting or intelligence gathering at mosques and local Muslim communities makes sense when the United States is at war with Islamic extremists.

Furthermore, a March 18, 2001, commentary in Time magazine by Krauthammer argued that racial and ethnic profiling in airports is an efficient way to help stop terrorists from traveling within the United States. Furthermore, some African Americans, who were usually against racial profiling as a group before the tragedy, took a different stance. For example, Omaha World-Herald African-American columnist Cliff Brunt (2001) expressed relief in having another ethnic group in the spotlight (Oct. 17, 2001). He wrote: "My people are not public enemy number one anymore. The names O.J. and Iron Mike don't fire people up the way they used to. The new bad guys are Muhammad and Osama" (p. 4).

Newspaper's Role in Society

Undeniably, newspapers are one of society's primary sources of information. Because the news coverage of major newspapers often sets the tone for coverage by other forms of media, it is imperative to question how reporters present information to the public. During the reporting process, journalists reproduce culturally embedded views of the world (Foucault, 1980) and use cultural codes to distinguish what is significant or valid and who has the standing to say what is true (Dickerson, 2003). This brings forth the question of newspaper frames.

Goffman (1974) coined the term "frame" to denote a technique of organization that enables individuals to "locate, perceive, identify, and label a seemingly infinite number of occurrences into something meaningful" (p. 21). He added that people use similar processes to frame an event—whether it is a drama, dance, newspaper story, political cartoon, or everyday conversation. On the most basic level, people create frames on a daily basis during conversations. For example, after a friend tells an interesting or controversial story, one might ask the race or age of a particular subject in the story. Upon hearing the person's race, he or she may frame the topic under discussion much differently based on the person's race. For instance, an African American individual might be more sympathetic toward a troubled teen-ager who's black, while a white person might be more sympathetic toward a troubled teenager who is white, or vice versa. As illustrated above, frames reflect judgments made by message creators or framers. In addition, some frames put information in either a positive or negative light, while others involve the simple alternative phrasing of terms.

What's more, Gitlin (1980) adapted these ideas to media framing, which he claims are a way journalists organize and package information and events for audiences. News frames serve several related functions in news texts. Most notably, they: 1) organize ideas upon which one may build a news story (Tankard 2001) 2) include certain aspects of a story while excluding others, and 3) propose an evaluative perspective to readers.

A Comparison of Newspaper Types: The Present Study

Researchers use various frameworks to look at the topics of race, class, and gender. One of the more effective methods is a comparison of communication styles across different social settings and years of time. The September 11 terrorist attacks, coupled with the issue of racial profiling and the different mission statements of black and mainstream media provide the perfect backdrop for such a media study. Using gatekeeping and framing theory, the researcher explored whether two related events—the September 11 attacks and the targeting of Arabs—led to any changes in the ways in which media outlets covered the issue of racial profiling. Framing theory focuses on how journalists organize information and the outcome of their interaction with their sources while promoting their own various perspectives. Gatekeeping theory, on the other hand, describes the role of initial selection and later editorial processing of event reports in news organizations.

To make the research manageable, the researcher confined the study to newspaper articles published during a specific period—three years before and three years after September 11. The sample included black and mainstream newspapers from Chicago, Los Angeles, New York, Philadelphia, and Atlanta, which have vital black press newspapers. Furthermore, the researcher used interpretive framing packages analysis to study the dynamics at play in black and mainstream media's coverage of racial profiling before and after September 11. Gamson and Lasch (1983) identify interpretive framing packages as containing core frames and framing devices that structure the same issue in different ways. Researchers noted that these ideas or "issue packages" do not infer whether individuals take a pro or con position on a topic, but rather allow for a range of positions concerning a particular issue.

Chicago Defender Executive Director Roland Martin provides an illustration of framing differences in black and mainstream newspapers in an August 16, 2005, article in which he explains how black press and mainstream media describe the same stories through different lenses. He writes, "But just today, while looking at CNN, I came across the Associated Press's report on the public viewing of Johnson [John H. Johnson]. They reported, hundreds of people filed past the Ebony and Jet founder's casket on Sunday, six days after his death at age 87. . . . In contrast to mainstream media's coverage, the Chicago Defender's Monday edition reported that more than 2,000 mourners paid their respects to the legendary media giant" (p. 3). Martin adds the following:

> You would have read this one line at the end of their Aug. 9 news briefs: Died: John H. Johnson, 87, publisher of Ebony and Jet magazines, in Chicago. The man [Johnson] spent 60 years building a business from $500 to $500 million, donated personally and through his companies more than $100 million and all he could merit in the one national newspaper dedicated to business is one funky line? Yet, if you read the Chicago Defender, you would have read 16 separate stories, columns, editorials, and seen countless pictorials celebrating his life. Same story. Different set of eyes. Different mission. Different result. In the words of the founders of the first black newspaper, Freedom's Journal, we must plead our own cause. (p. 3)

Based on findings from previous studies, the researcher speculated that the interpretive packages journalists used at both black and mainstream newspapers would be different due to the varied missions addressed by the two newspaper types. Mainstream media aims to serve the general population, while the black press targets the black community. In addition, black press newspapers often cover specific issues important to the black community from a black perspective that is often overlooked by the mainstream media.

Although occurrences of overt racism in news stories appear to be few, studies have shown that African-American and general press outlets handle stories differently. For instance, in their study of black and mainstream newspapers published in 1894, Ratzlaff and Iorio (1994) found that while both newspaper types often focused on the same issues, they did not use the same frames. To illustrate this point, the black press newspaper in their study framed the labor issue by its impact on black people, while the mainstream newspaper framed it as an issue that touches the lives of people from all walks of life. The study also found that positions advocated by the black and mainstream newspapers tended to follow party lines with the mission statements of the individual newspapers serving as a key factor that influenced how journalists framed those issues. Furthermore, the mainstream newspaper acknowledged its political association with the Republican Party, while the black press newspaper identified itself as a newspaper aimed at black citizens in its city.

Previous Racial Profiling Framing Studies

Other September 11 media studies have alluded to some interesting findings. For example, in their study of how 25 regional and national newspapers talked about "racial profiling" for the five months before and after September 11, Domke, et al. (2003) found that before September 11, eighty-two percent of sources focused on police behavior and two percent focused on terrorism. After the event, thirty-three percent focused on terrorism and twenty-seven percent on policing. In reference to source types, findings showed that most Arab American and African American sources were individuals rather than government officials or non-government opinion leaders. The scholars found that the media quoted Arab Americans from political interest groups, but it did not cite African Americans in the same capacity.

Li and Izard (2003) found that newspapers and television networks framed their coverage of the September 11 tragedy differently. For example, human-interest framing was more prominent in newspapers than in network coverage. Television placed priority on informing the public of what was happening, and human interest was a prominent frame only during the later stage of networks' coverage. Furthermore, the top frames selected by both print and TV media reflected the same major theme—i.e., a terrorist attack that bore a political identity and a tragedy that involved the whole nation; however, no other differences were evident among the five television networks and among the eight newspapers in their sample.

In another example, Gandy and Baruh (2005) identified the frames writers used most frequently in editorials and letters to the editor published between January 1, 1994, and March 19, 1999. They found that sixty-six percent of all the items reviewed tended to frame the issue as an institutional problem, with thirty-one percent characterizing it as a problem for society as a whole. Additionally, an analysis of headlines and lead paragraphs indicated that the majority, forty-two percent, of these items framed the problem in terms of "black loss" or hardship, with thirty-five percent including statistics about the number of drivers stopped, searched, or arrested as part of the thematic frame.

This study moves beyond previous works by looking at the frames used by black versus mainstream newspapers before and after September 11.

Black Press Vs. Mainstream Media

A study of this nature is of interest because founders created black press newspapers to provide a voice for African Americans, and as a result, different perspectives have developed in response to oppression or misrepresentation of minorities in mainstream newspapers. Therefore, the comparison of mainstream with minority media should yield a rich study of the processes of interpretation and representation of cultural identities because media resources produced by and for minorities provide interpretations of events and identities that run counter to mainstream representations (Squires, 2002).

The differences in the coverage of racial profiling by black and mainstream newspapers are important because frames often shape public perceptions of political issues or institutions (Semetko & Valkenburg, 2000). For example, research has shown that whites often form their opinions on race relations based on the media (Domke, et al., 2003). In addition, the types of frames used are significant because the framing of an issue is often a strategic means to attract more supporters and to mobilize collective actions.

Though research has documented differences, not many studies have analyzed how tragedies deeply entrenched in one or both communities influence the frames of black and mainstream media in their coverage of various issues. Of particular interest is whether a tragedy can make newspapers change their overall missions in their coverage of an issue. September 11 provided a platform on which one might make a comparison. Theoretically, the tragedy might make the two media types change how they covered the issue of racial profiling because following September 11, many journalists banned together for the common good of protecting American citizens from terrorists.

Study Overview

In summary, the present study builds upon the framing and gatekeeping literature to examine how mainstream and African-American newspapers framed the phenomena of "racial profiling" three years before and three years after the September 11 terrorist attacks to assess if it made a significant difference. The study looks at three areas: 1) the frames and catchphrases reporters chose to cover racial profiling, 2) emphasis or perceived importance of the issue, 3) sources and ethnic groups journalists highlighted in the coverage of racial profiling.

Sociologists and criminal justice researchers have studied the subject of racial profiling for more than a decade; however, they have done little in reference to the media's coverage of the controversial topic. The influx of articles about racial profiling and Arab Americans provides the perfect backdrop for such a study. The terrorist attacks created a daunting environment in which both African-American and mainstream reporters felt threatened.

Such a study is merited because newspaper articles provide historical content that may be used to analyze mistakes made by the media in covering various issues. This type of analysis may be used to help reporters improve their reporting strategies and to head off the repetition of mistakes.

Chapter Two: Review of the Literature of September 11

On September 11, 2001, around 8:46 a.m., nineteen men simultaneously hijacked four U.S. domestic commercial airliners. The terrorists crashed two planes into the World Trade Center in Manhattan; a third plane into the Pentagon in Arlington County, Virginia; and the fourth into a rural field in Somerset County, Pennsylvania. The official count records 2,986 deaths in the attacks. The continuous coverage by television networks of the aggressive terrorist attacks began within minutes of the first plane crash into the North Tower of the World Trade Center (Li & Izard, 2003). Journalists had no time for special preparations; undeniably, they had little time even to adequately think through the alternatives before the event forced them to make decisions about strategies. As a result, broadcast and Internet journalists framed the news stories as the experience unfolded, while daily newspapers that did not publish a special edition on the same day had an evening to ponder their strategies before delivering accounts of the event the next morning.

Thanks to the media, Americans knew about the tragedy within minutes and racial profiling became a key focal point in coverage of the topic. Viewpoints about the controversial human rights topic changed for many people after

September 11. Before the terrorist attacks, it appeared that much of mainstream America agreed that racial profiling was wrong. However, after the tragedy, the issue became debatable. For instance, the Department of Justice asked Congress for additional surveillance procedures, relating specifically to the use of wiretaps on telephones and computers (Brennen, 2002). In addition, then-Attorney General John Ashcroft pushed for the expansion of governmental power in order to prevent future terrorist attacks.

Additionally, polls provide evidence for vast fluctuations in beliefs. For instance, a 1999 Gallup Poll found that 80 percent or more of both white and black Americans were against racial profiling, while after September 11 polls provided evidence that people began to favor it. For example, a Boston Globe poll found that African Americans were more likely than other racial groups to support profiling and stringent airport security checks for Arabs and Arab Americans (Scales, 2001). Additionally, a Gallup Poll found that 71 percent of African Americans—as opposed to 51 percent of whites—believed Arabs and Arab Americans should undergo special, more intensive security checks before boarding airplanes.

September 11 and Its Aftermath

Violence against Middle Easterners and Muslims heated up across the country after September 11. In fact, agencies reported more than one thousand bias incidents against Arabs, Muslims, and South Asians during the weeks following the tragedy. These crimes included damage to businesses, homes, and places of worship as well as harassment by law enforcers. Not surprisingly, September 11 increased national awareness of the potential for terrorism, and the stance the government took during the aftermath of September 11 ignited a broad range of reactions. For example, federal officials arrested hundreds of Arab and Muslim aliens, then questioned, detained, and deported many of them. Officials subjected others to special registration procedures. Also, in the first two years after September 11, the United States created immigration laws that, by design, applied almost exclusively to Arabs, Muslims, and South Asians. The final regulation issued in August 2002, required all male non-citizens over the age of sixteen from twenty-five countries to report to the local Immigration and Naturalization Service (INS) office for registration and fingerprinting (Chon & Artz, 2005).

A year-long study conducted by the Domestic Human Rights Program of Amnesty International USA found that the unlawful use of race in police, immigration, and airport security procedures expanded tremendously after the terrorist attacks of September 11, 2001. Furthermore, findings showed that racial profiling of citizens and visitors of Middle Eastern and South Asian descent, and others who appear to be from these areas or members of the Muslim and Sikh faiths increased substantially after September 11, 2001. Examples of individual cases vary. For instance, fear of additional terrorist attacks led to the removal of more than a dozen brown-skinned men from flights throughout the country because passengers thought they were from the Middle East (Polakow-Suransky, 2001). In another example, authorities prohibited a U.S. citizen of Egyptian origin to board a United Airlines flight in Tampa, Florida on September 21. An airport manager told him apologetically that the pilot refused to fly with him on board because his name was Mohamed (Polakow-Suransky, 2001). In a similar case, pilots diverted a Northwest Airlines flight from Memphis to Las Vegas to Arkansas after the crew reported suspicious behavior on the part of two passengers (National Review, Oct. 14, 2002). South Asian men boarded the flight at the last minute, would not take their seats, and spent an unusual amount of time in the plane's bathroom. According to the article, their explanation turned out to be innocent; the men had spent an unplanned night in Memphis after missing a connection, and they wanted to shave, which they had not been able to do in their hotel.

In another example, on September 13, three young Middle Eastern men sped through a tollbooth on I-75 in the Everglades in Florida (National Review, Oct. 14, 2002). Police stopped the car after tracking the license plate number because someone overheard the men in a Georgia restaurant talking threateningly about September 11. The article said they were uncooperative when questioned. However, the suspects were actually medical students from Chicago who drove to Florida to complete a practical-studies assignment in Miami. Although the person who reported them stands by the story, they denied talking about September 11 (National Review, Oct. 14, 2002).

Nailing Down a Group

The government's directive to register Middle Eastern men using photographs and fingerprints (Goldberg, 2002) was not an easy task because the "race" under scrutiny is a hodgepodge of different groups, including Muslims, religious affiliations, and various ethnicities such as South Asian, Indonesian, and Arabs. According to the 2000 United States Census, of the 281.4 million people in the United States, 1.2 million reported an Arab ancestry. Arabs were one of 33 ancestry groups with populations of more than 1 million in the United States (De la Cruz & Brittingham, 2003). Most of the people included in the count had ancestries originating from Arabic-speaking countries. For instance, a person is included in the Arab ancestry category if he or she reports being one of the following: Arab, Egyptian, Iraqi, Jordanian, Lebanese, Middle Eastern, Moroccan, North African, Palestinian, Syrian, and so on. However, De la Cruz and Brittingham (2003) caution that that some people from these countries may not consider themselves Arab, and conversely, some people who consider themselves Arab may not be included in this definition such as Mauritanian, Somalian, Djiboutian, Sudanese, and Comoros Islander. On the other hand, Kurds and Berbers who do not usually consider themselves Arab were included in this category for consistency with the 1990 census and census 2000 data products.

Identifying groups by religion also presented a problem for officials after September 11. For example, Arabs and Muslims are often lumped together but are fundamentally different identity groups. In fact, the majority of Arabs in the United States are Christian, and Arabs constitute a minority of Muslims worldwide (Chon & Artz, 2005). Because census reports do not track religious affiliations, the number of Muslims in the United States is difficult to assess. The best estimate is six to seven million (Chon & Artz, 2005). The various ethnicities of Muslims also present a challenge. For example, many surveys indicate that more than two-thirds of persons of the Muslim faith are African American, and a study by the American Muslim Council indicates that blacks make up as much as one-half of all Muslims in the United States and are the fastest growing segment (Bellinger, 2002). The group's interpretation of Islam includes nationalistic and separatist theology that boasts of the virtues and superiority of the black race. For example, many of its followers believe the white race, through its own wickedness, faces impending extinction, and that the black man would one day rule the world (Bellinger, 2002).

For many of the members of the Nation of Islam, September 11 was a double-edged sword because they were now marginalized for reasons related to their religion, in addition to their race (Eisenberg, 2005). In a January 24, 2005, Newsday article Eisenberg provides this example of sentiments during this period. A young African-American Muslim who was asked what it's like living in America after September 11, responded: "It's like being black—twice."

Interestingly, it appears that Americans were able to distinguish between religion and ethnicities when forming their opinions following the September 11 terrorist attacks. In fact, according to polls conducted by the Pew Forum on Religion and Public Life and the Pew Research Center for the People and the Press, opinions of Muslims did not suffer in the wake of terrorist attacks. A majority of Americans (55 percent) said they had a favorable opinion of Muslim Americans. The number was roughly the same proportion that expressed positive opinions of Muslim Americans in Pew surveys conducted in July 2003 and March 2002 and significantly higher than the 45 percent holding favorable views in March 2001, prior to the September 11 terrorist attacks. Also worth noting, is in the wake of later terrorist attacks in London, the number of Americans who believed that Islam is more likely than other religions to encourage violence fell to 36 percent from 44 percent (Keeter, 2005).

Such opinions might be based on facts. According to the U.S. Department of Justice, in 2002 the FBI recorded eight terrorist incidents in the United States and its territories that were carried out by domestic terrorists, and animal rights and environmental extremists (Terrorism 1999/2000). In 2001, the FBI reported that domestic terrorists carried out twelve of the recorded fourteen terrorist incidents in the United States and its territories; and at the time of the report, authorities had not characterized the unsolved series of anthrax-tainted letters sent through the U.S. Postal Service as either domestic or international in nature. According to the report, international terrorists carried out the final attack—September 11, 2001.

More recently, the primary perpetrators of terrorism in the Western Hemisphere have been narcoterrorist, or organizations based in Colombia and the remnants of radical leftist Andean groups, according to the 2005 Country Reports on Terrorism. The report also states that with the exception of the United States and Canada, there were no known operational cells of Islamic terrorists in the hemisphere, although scattered pockets of ideological supporters and facilitators in South America and the Caribbean lent various types of support to terrorist groups in the Middle East.

Middle Easterners and the Media Post-September 11

Some Arab leaders blame journalists for the alleged anti-Arab sentiment in the United States. According to Said (2001), since September 11, an organized media campaign imposes the Israeli vision of the world on Americans, with practically nothing to counter it. The main themes of this school of thought are Islam and the Arabs are the true causes of terrorism; Israel has been facing such terrorism all its life, and Arafat and Bin Laden are the same thing. Moreover, he asserts that most U.S. Arab allies, especially Egypt and Saudi Arabia, have played a clear negative role in sponsoring anti-Americanism, supporting terrorism, and maintaining corrupt societies. American people thought the terrorist activities could only come from one source and that would be the Arabs and the Muslims, Abdalla said (Moss, 2001, p.1).

Although stereotypes existed prior to September 11, Arabs were more often invisible in the Western press. In fact, researchers, in general, have found the media ignored them all together; when not ignored, they are usually presented unfavorably. For example, Merskin (2004) writes that popular culture and the mass media in the United States have generated and sustained stereotypes of a monolithic evil Arab, depicting all Muslims as Arab and all Arabs as terrorists. The frame of reference with which Americans perceive Middle Easterners today began forming in the mid-19th century when Western historians, geographers, ethnographers, and Western Christian missionaries visited Palestine. They conveyed their impressions of the land and its peoples to readers and congregations in Europe and America (Christison, 1997). Arabs first gained national attention in the late 1890s and early 1900s when immigrants began appearing in mainstream publications (Pulcini, 1993). Initially characterized as peddlers and beggars, Arabs soon became the villains of choice for the motion picture industry (Shaheen, 1984). Historians speculate that the stereotype of Arabs that began with Rudolph Valentino in "The Sheik" has developed into the transnational villain of television and film and culture in general (Barsamian, 2001). Establishing such otherness has historically been a fluid undertaking applicable to any number of racialized groups (Ali, 2003). Although Americans probably did not have a clearly defined perception of Arabs, they used their exposure through the mass media to form a vague sense of Arabs as distasteful (Christison, 1997).

Even today, the media usually portray Arabs on TV or in movies as evil or foolish. Hollywood movies both reflect and perpetuate these stereotypes: Arabs are often villains or financial backers of espionage. For example, plots as in "The Seige," which portrays the U.S. military declaring martial law and imprisoning American Muslims and Arab Americans following a series of terrorist bombings. In addition, the "Mummy" included negative stereotypes such as the comment: "I'll trade you my two sisters for a camel" (Saito, 2001). By using such representations in news, movies, and magazine stories, the media have fostered the construction of an evil Arab stereotype that includes a wide variety of people, ideas, and religions (Merskin, 2004; Shaheen, 1984). These negative portrayals and stereotypes coupled with the circumstances surrounding September 11 add to the noteworthiness of this study.

Racial Profiling Evolution

While the coverage of September 11 and its influence on the understanding of racial profiling is a trend spurred by the attacks, the topic has been controversial in the United States since the late 1990s when the issue emerged. From a historical perspective, researchers speculate that the term "racial profiling" originated following studies focusing on the New Jersey Turnpike in the early 1990s when law enforcers labeled the turnpike the main conduit for the shipment of illegal drugs and other contraband to the criminal markets of the Northeast (Derbyshire, 2001). The term "racial profiling" appears to have further developed around April of 1998, when two white New Jersey state troopers pulled over a van for speeding. As the officers approached the van from behind, an African American driver suddenly reversed toward them. The troopers fired shots from their handguns, wounding three of the van's four occupants, all of whom were black or Hispanic. The troopers, James Kenna and John Hogan, instantly became household names associated with "racial profiling." Other sources speculate that the media did not begin to label such crimes as "racial profiling" until Al Gore debated Bill Bradley at New York's Apollo Theatre in February of 2000. During this nationally televised debate, Bradley, spoke of the 1999 New York police officers' shooting of African immigrant Amadou Diallo. Shortly thereafter, the term became a commonly used household catchphrase (Derbyshire, 2001).

Another case that catapulted racial profiling into the media spotlight was the beating of Rodney King; an African-American motorist whom Los Angeles police attacked repeatedly while a bystander videotaped the incident (Ali, 2003). Although King actually broke the law, the incident did not play well on national television. Audiences viewed the videotape daily until the case ultimately ended up in state court where a judge charged the four officers with using excessive force in subduing King. Later, a jury acquitted the four men. As to be expected, the police officers' acquittal raised a public outcry for many people, especially those from the African-American community, who believed that the well-publicized beating was racially motivated, excessive, and an example of police brutality. The event led to the 1992 Los Angeles riots and protests around the world.

Figure 1. Racial Profiling Timeline

Date	Type	Description
1803-1805:	The Free Negro Registry	Implemented to identify and track so-called free persons of color. In colonial Virginia, such persons were required to show identification to any white person on demand.
1880:	Jim Crow Laws	Statutes enacted in the 1880s by Southern states and municipalities that legalized segregation between blacks and whites. Historians believe the name is derived from a character in a popular minstrel song.
1865:	Black Codes And Vagrancy Laws	Regulated civil and legal rights ranging from marriage to the right to hold and sell property. In many states, if unemployed, blacks faced the potential of being arrested and charged with vagrancy.
1941:	Japanese Internment Camps	The forcible relocation of approximately 112,000 to 120,000 Japanese and Japanese Americans from the West Coast of the United States during World War II to hastily constructed housing facilities called "War Relocation Camps" in remote portions of the nation's interior. About 62 percent were United States citizens.
1990:	New Jersey Turnpike:	Nicknamed "White Man's Pass." According to reports, the New Jersey Highway Patrol considered the turnpike a popular route for drug traffickers. Officers stop a disproportionately large number of minorities on the turnpike.
1999:	Amadou Diallo	In February 1999, four New York City policemen searching for a rape suspect knocked on Amadou Diallo's door to question him. When he came to the door he reached inside his jacket for his wallet. Officers shot at him 41 times, hitting him with 19 bullets.

Although the name itself became popular much later, racial and ethnic profiling has had a long history in the United States (see Figure 1). The Free Negro Registry is an example of how whites used racial profiling as a means of identifying and tracking so-called Free Persons of Color (Willis, 2003). In colonial Virginia, law enforcers required all free persons of color to show identification to any white person on demand. After the Civil War, in 1880, authorities revived old laws and renamed them Jim Crow laws after a black minstrel character. Another example occurred during after the Reconstruction years in the South. White vigilantes kept peremptory watch over African Americans (Coke, 2003), using the Black Codes and vagrancy laws to legitimize their actions (Foner, 1998). The internment camps after the Japanese attack on Pearl Harbor in 1941 is yet another example; federal authorities forced 120,000 men, women, and children of Japanese ancestry into camps, equating ethnicity with guilt (Mark, 2003). The camps were a direct result of the Supreme Court ruling in Korematsu versus United States, which mandated that anyone of Japanese descent and residing on the Pacific coast of the United States could be presumed a traitor and placed in prisoner-of-war camps.

The modern day racial profiling of blacks and Hispanics grew out of the war on drugs, which President Ronald Reagan kicked off in 1982 with the establishment of a task force to increase air and sea operations in order to reduce drug smuggling in the South Florida area (Harris, 1999). However, in 1985, the Florida Department of Motor Vehicle issued procedures for identifying the common characteristics of drug couriers. The guidelines admonished troopers to be suspicious of rental cars, scrupulous obedience to traffic laws, and drivers wearing lots of gold, or who do not fit the vehicle, and ethnic groups associated with the drug trade. Based on this information, state troopers often initiated traffic stops using race-based profiles (Harris, 1999).

Harris (1999) adds that the drug war heated up with the emergence of crack cocaine in the spring of 1986. Press accounts of inner-city crack use fostered a phase of intense public concern about illegal drugs and helped reinforce the impression that drug use was chiefly a minority problem. Enforcement of the nation's drug laws at the street level focused on poor communities of color. For example, Operation Pressure Point in New York attempted to free the primarily Hispanic Lower East Side of the drug trade. Other efforts included Operation Hammer in Los Angeles, Operation Invincible in Memphis, Operation Clean Sweep in Chicago, and the Red Dog Squad in Atlanta (Harris, 1999). According to police reports, nationwide, arrests for drug possession reported by state and local police nearly doubled from 400,000 in 1981 to 762,718 in 1988. Minorities represented a disproportionate number in these figures (Harris, 1999). The controversy surrounding racial profiling originates not from past evidence of deliberate abuse of the police tactic, but rather from police officers' over-reliance on race as an indicator of criminal activity (Gandy & Baruh, 2005). In reality, it is among a number of diverse types of criminal profiling. For example, police may engage in a process of systematically pooling collective police experience into information that is comprehensive in order to identify potential criminals. Experts have developed profiles of serial killers, child molesters, and tax evaders (Gandy & Baruh, 2005).

By the mid-1990s police and lawmakers began to acknowledge the existence of racial profiling (Coke, 2003). According to polls, the American public was aware of the inappropriateness of profiling. In 2000, a survey of approximately 80 percent of Americans indicated that they had heard of racial profiling and had expressed the opinion that it should stop at this time. The Civil Rights

Division of the U.S. Department of Justice began to sue police departments where it found patterns and practices of racial and ethnic profiling (Coke, 2003).

Today, the Harvard Civil Rights-Civil Liberties Law Review outlines three schools of thought that have dominated the racial profiling debate for the last decade. The first group, which includes civil rights and social movement organizations, such as the American Civil Liberties Union and the National Association for the Advancement of Colored People, opposes racial profiling altogether. Members of this group base their argument on the idea that such searches are illegal and unproductive. The second group, police administrators and officers, often support race and ethnically targeted vehicle searches by police based on the argument that such searches are more likely to reveal illegal dealings such as drug and firearm possession. The third group, judges and constitutional commentators, use technical dissection to resolve legal challenges to racial profiling. For example, they distinguish between the Fourth Amendment, which guarantees protection against unreasonable searches, and the Fourteenth Amendment's guarantee of equal treatment, and largely relegate the use of race in policing to the latter (Harvard Civil Rights-Civil Liberties Law Review, 2004).

History of Racial Profiling In Sample Cities

Instances of racial profiling were common in the sample cities. For example, in New York, Police Commissioner Raymond Kelly barred racial profiling in a March 2002 order. The New York City Council and Mayor Bloomberg negotiated the bill titled "Kelly's ban" to prohibit officers and other law enforcement agents employed by the city from using race, ethnicity, religion, or national origin as the determinate factor for law enforcement actions. Enforcers enacted the law following allegations of police misconduct after the torture of Abner Louima, who was arrested outside a nightclub in 1997 and later sodomized with a broken broomstick; and the police shooting of Amadou Diallo, an unarmed West African immigrant whom police shot in front of his apartment complex.

Meanwhile in Chicago during 2000, the city council passed an ordinance prohibiting racial profiling by the Chicago Police Department, or any other law enforcement agency operating within the city limits. The proposal attempted to address concerns over civil rights violations raised by numerous cases of alleged racial profiling uncovered across the United States. In 2006, data showed that officers in Chicago stopped minority drivers at a rate 15 percent higher than their driving-age population. In addition, CPD officers stopped African-American drivers at a rate 29 percent higher than their driving-age population (Yohnka, 2006). What is more, police reported that minority drivers were three times more likely to consent to a vehicle search than non-minorities. Also in Chicago, similar problems existed in Arab communities after September 11. For example, newspapers reported fifty-five hate crimes and at least once an angry mob descended on a mosque (Yohnka, 2006).

Similarly, in Philadelphia, in a study of all 23 police districts, the American Civil Liberties Union found that police stopped blacks far more often than they stopped whites. Blacks make up 42 percent of Philadelphia's population, according to a 1995 Census data, but accounted for 60 percent of all stops. Whites, who make up 54 percent of the population, accounted for only 36 percent of all stops, the report said. Furthermore, a report found that police stopped and detained 36 percent of all minorities without legal justification. In an effort to curb racial profiling, the Philadelphia Police Department began requiring detailed reports of all stops. In addition, a federal court order now required police to fill out both sides of a special form for every citizen contact.

Likewise, in Washington, D.C., in March of 2001, the Metropolitan Police Department made public that its officers had exchanged e-mails containing racist, sexist, and homophobic language about one another and other citizens (Citizen Complaint Review Board, 2002). The announcement raised concerns about police prejudice and racial profiling. Almost ten months after the department announced it would take steps to limit racial profiling, personnel had not developed an operating data collection system.

A Look at the Media

Mainstream press is often identified as targeting the general population with the intent to provide continuous objective coverage of issues and areas of interest. For the purpose of this study, mainstream media denotes news outlets that produce content specifically conceived and designed to reach and appeal to a large audience. Some researchers view the mass media audience as forming a mass society with a lack of social connections such as race, gender, etc. Adding to this definition, the American Heritage Dictionary defines mainstream as representing the prevalent attitudes, values, and practices of a society or group. For example, mainstream morality would denote morality as seen by a majority of people in society. In addition, mainstream media have the duty to address concerns by the general public, according to the Project for Excellence in Journalism. It is through news and media that people learn about the world beyond their direct experiences (The State of the News Media Annual Report on American Journalism, 2004). Furthermore, the Statement of Shared Purpose written by journalists involved with the Project for Excellence in Journalism states: "The central purpose of journalism is to provide citizens with accurate and reliable information they need to function in a free society" (p. 1). The statement also emphasizes journalism's loyalty to citizens and the larger public good as well as its role as a watchdog and its responsibility to offer a voice to the voiceless.

In contrast to mainstream media, Dates and Barlow (1993) define black press as newspapers and magazines aimed at African-American readers that speak to their issues. Fellows (1998) writes that the community spirit that motivates so many African-American newspapers today draws on a 170-year legacy of journalistic activism. Publishers founded the first black newspapers to spread the word against slavery. Blacks did not trust white editors to champion their causes so they started newspapers of their own such as Freedom's Journal, founded in 1827, and Ram's Horn and Frederick Douglass' The North Star, both founded in 1847. After the Civil War, hundreds of black newspapers sprang up to inform, educate, and to agitate (Fellows, 1998).

According to Dates and Barlow (1993), prior to the creation of the African-American press, many African Americans believed they had no voice in the general press unless their views mirrored those of the dominant culture. This is of interest because of the small numbers of African Americans who work in the mainstream media. For example, Weaver and Wilhoit (1996) found in their study of American journalists that, as of 1992, only 3.7 percent of all full-time journalists working for mainstream media were African American. Because of these statistics, the issue of fair representation in print media is a tangible reason for concern. Questions that often emerge when considering the issue of mainstream media's coverage of minorities include: Does the majority press employ a representative number of minority journalists? Does the majority press provide adequate minority participation at most decision-making or management levels? Finally, does the majority press present African American news in a bias fashion? These questions may not be addressed with diverse newsrooms, according to Gandy (1998), who asserts that even if newspapers manage to hire minority journalists, that alone will not guarantee a more honest and representative brand of reporting. He adds that stories by journalists of all colors reflect the dominant newsroom values, which dictate similar coverage of events by minority and non-minority news-people. In support of this notion, Gans (1979) used the ethnocentrism value theory to explain why mass media cover their own state's policy or action in a positive image and cover the enemy state negatively if the two countries have different opinions about the same issue. It may also apply to issues of race. In all likelihood, news coverage by organizations that are racially diverse may still reflect the attitudes of contemporary racism.

Dates and Pease (1994) assert that the norm in this country is that the perspectives of white, mainstream men generally create the lenses through which America—whether peripherally or directly—views race and itself. Tuchman (1978) observed, "News is a window on the world. Through its frame, Americans learn of themselves and others, of their institutions, leaders, and lifestyles, and those of the other nations and their peoples" (p.1). This led her to the developmental concept: the "news net," which she defines as a figurative mesh that is cast over a coverage area to capture news items. However, it is an image of an old, worn-out net in which the holes are uneven: some are larger than others. She asserts that if the holes in the mesh are too large, a lot of non-mainstream or alternative information slips through. That is, a lot of news about blacks is simply not captured by the traditional news net.

Hall's idea of a "racist common sense" extends Tuchman's news net to coverage of minorities. According to the researcher, the media without question use this method as they filter information through a white worldview (Hall, 1980). Moreover, research findings consistently indicate that African Americans have a strong belief that the mainstream media is white because composite television news images feed racial stereotypes, encouraging white hostility and fear of African Americans (Entman, 1994). Frequently absent from the mass media is the examination of issues from the viewpoints of African Americans.

Chapter Three: Theoretical Framework

The most prominent conceptual framework for this study is framing. The theory coupled with the gatekeeper theory provided a foundation for the researcher to research the issue of black and mainstream media's coverage of racial profiling before and after September 11. The basis of framing theory presumes the prevalent media will focus attention on newsworthy events and place them within a sphere of meaning, and that media professionals create frames in the context of complex organizations. Further, scholars assert that a framing effect occurs when, in the course of describing an issue or event, a speaker's emphasis on a subset of potentially relevant considerations causes individuals to focus on these considerations when constructing their opinions (Druckman, 2001). Framing arises in almost every instance where the media present an event or piece of information thought worthy of transmission to the public from any angle.

Furthermore, Gamson (1988) defines "framing" as answering the question, "What is the basic source of controversy or concern in this issue?" (p. 165). While working within a complex news culture, journalists strive to be objective; however, according to Gans (1979), it is impossible for anyone to work in any environment without values, which he suggests in the news industry may manifest themselves as subjectivity in coverage. Similarly, gatekeeping theory describes the role of initial selection and later editorial processing of event reports in news organizations.

The gatekeeper approach (Tuchman, 1978) is pertinent to the study of portrayals of Arabs/Middle Easterners in the media because race and culture play a key role in what reporters and editors perceive as important. Undoubtedly, gatekeepers at mainstream media and black press outlets will have a different idea or perception of what is important and what journalists should cover in their respective newspapers.

MEDIA FRAMES: A CLOSER LOOK

The Role of Frames

Frames provide a means through which one can study different aspects of an issue. Entman (1991) asserts that the media have the ability to enlarge an idea, to draw attention to it, or to shrink an idea in order to diminish the coverage of it. Furthermore, Entman (1991) explains that news frames help establish the literal common sense interpretation of events. Furthermore, frames allow organizations and policy makers to disseminate messages. For example, when two parties represent opposing viewpoints, Gamson, Crouteau, Hoynes and Sasson (1992) suggest they become engaged in a frame contest. In such contests, success or failure rests upon whether a person's preferred interpretations gain prominence in media and acceptance by audiences. The factors that influence the longevity of frames, Gamson and Modligiani (1989) pointed out, are the activities of non-media sponsors of frames, who want to advance frames they find useful; media practices that reflect working norms, routines and values of journalists; and cultural resonance. If frames resonate with larger cultural themes, they increase in appeal.

What is more, framing allows elites to exert power over the public. News articles containing frames help the ideas of those in power become the basis of public opinion. This is a critical concept when analyzing news coverage of controversial issues that the average reader will likely encounter through the media. Assessing the frame of an article can provide an insight into the role that media texts play in society and in politics. In addition, the theory of framing helps explain how the media work. Media frames are "persistent patterns of cognition, interpretation, and presentation, of section, emphasis, and exclusion" (Gitlin, 1980, p. 7). Entman (1993) summarized the essence of framing processes with the following:

> Framing essentially involves selection and salience. To frame is to elect some aspects of perceived reality and make them more salient in the communicating text, in such a way as to promote a particular problem definition, causal interpretation, moral evaluation, and/or treatment recommendation for the item described. Frames, then, define problems—determine what a causal agent is doing and costs

and benefits usually measured in terms of cultural values; diagnose causes—identify the forces creating the problem; make moral judgments—evaluate causal agents and their effects; and suggest remedies—offer and justify treatments for the problem and predict their likely effects. (p. 55)

Reese (1997) posits that frames meaningfully structure the social world and society's understanding of social phenomena by determining what content is relevant and by influencing the symbolic representation of a topic, including language use, sentence structure, and "code words."

Figure 2: Framing Flow Chart

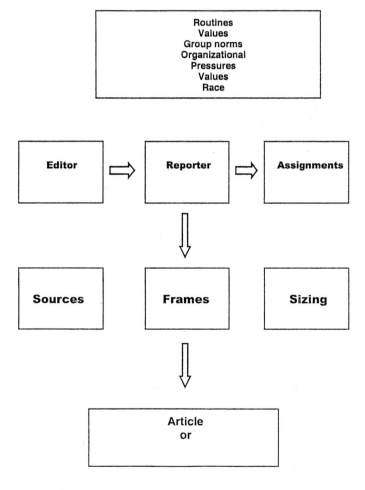

Media Message

Frames provide a means through which one can study different aspects of a topic because it usually occurs when one can present an issue using a variety of packages or thematic slants. For example, a "pro-life frame" will use terms such as baby, abortionist, unborn, murder, and so on whereas the "pro-choice frame" might use fetus, doctor, woman, and freedom to describe the same situation (Hertog & McLeod, 1999).

Additionally, framing theory looks at how journalists organize information and the outcome of their interaction with their sources while promoting their own various perspectives. Framing is an "ideological contest" that looks at the scope of an issue and the parties that are influential in determining the values that are relevant to that particular issue (Pan & Kosicki, 2001).

A growing list of researchers has examined coverage of social problems from a media framing perspective. For example, theorists often use framing to analyze press coverage of issues such as affirmative action (Gamson & Modigliani, 1987), spousal abuse (Messner & Solomon, 1992), and other weighty subject matter. Such studies generally support the idea that journalists and editors select, package, disseminate news, and mediate it through organizational processes and ideologies (Watkins, 2001). For instance, Gans (1979) points out that in the newsgathering processes of mainstream media, journalists cannot avoid the unthinkable practice of bringing their personal values with them when they decide what constitutes news and how to present that news.

Frames and Sizing

As mentioned earlier, this study looks at three main areas of framing; one of the more important areas is sizing/emphasis or perceived importance of the issue. The essence of framing according to Entman (1991) is sizing, or to what extent a communicator magnifies or miniaturizes any depicted reality and thus, makes it more or less significant. According to previous studies, one can assess the event's importance by how much material is available and its prominence. Graber (1988) noted that readers of traditional newspapers use importance cues such as location, visual size, and story length provided by editors to guide their decisions in selecting news articles.

When considering sizing or emphasis, framing essentially involves selection and salience. Whether consciously or subconsciously, a communicator, or journalist, provides salience to some ideas over others. Readers then look to these texts and walk away with the ideas that are most salient, and they understand these based on the understanding they have of words and symbols within their own cultural sphere. Here framing involves a reciprocal relationship between the reader and the text, which is a two-way exercise (St. Clair & Tajima, 2003). Not surprisingly, studies have shown that the African American periodical press agenda contributed significantly to African American perceptions of salient issues.

Sources in the Media

Another important area in this study is sources. Previous studies have found that frames manifest themselves in a reporter's selection of sources and quotes. For instance, reporters may use sources effectively as framing devices by creating the illusion of validity or factuality, or by adding credibility to certain points of view (Pan & Kosicki, 1993). In the end, reporters can add weight to a point of view by quoting official sources or marginalize certain points of view by relating a quote or point of view to a social deviant. This relationship is give-and-take. Policy actors require the media to highlight their messages in the public eye, while the media need political elites to serve as spokespersons in order to fill news holes and to provide interest. Druckman (2001) conducted two laboratory experiments to test the prediction that framing requires a presumably credible source. The results suggest that a credible source can use a frame to alter the perceived importance of different considerations. In contrast, a perceived noncredible source cannot use a frame to alter opinions. Druckman concluded, "Perceived source credibility appears to be a prerequisite for successful framing. . . . Framing effects may occur not because elites seek to manipulate citizens, but rather because citizens delegate to credible elites for guidance" (p. 225).

Framing and Interpretive Packages

The researcher attempted to identify frames using research methods by Gamson and Lasch (1983) who identified two primary parts of interpretive packages: 1) the core of the frame, which organizes the central idea of the issue, 2) signature elements, which include two categories—framing and reasoning devices. The two identified framing elements as metaphors, exemplars, catchphrases, depictions, and visual images. Entman (1991) further explains through keywords, metaphors, concepts, symbols, and visual images emphasized in a news narrative, a salient idea is easier to understand and easier to remember than other ideas. Furthermore, Gamson and Lasch (1983) contend that the ideas that appear in news are best understood as media packages that feature a central organizing idea for events and employ various framing or symbolic devices that support the main idea of the story.

According to the two, the task of media workers is to arrange random events into a meaningful, organized interpretive package.

News frames are almost entirely implicit and taken for granted. They do not appear to either journalists or audiences as social constructions but as primary attributes of events that reporters are merely reflecting. News frames make the world look natural. They define what is selected, what is excluded, what is emphasized. In short, news presents a packaged world, and not all of the recesses of the package are visible (p. 80).

Gamson and Modigliani (1989) suggest that several major factors shape how the media frame the news. For instance, theme represents the main idea in a package and connects different elements of a story such as descriptors of action, or actor, quotes, sources, and background information. Cultural resonance refers to the degree that journalists package news in accordance with the beliefs, myths, stories, folk tales, and imagery that coincide with the dominant culture of a society.

What About Objectivity?

Critics often pan journalistic framing for its bias and lack of objectivity (Hackett, 1985). Because journalistic frames do not develop in a vacuum but are sponsored by multiple social actors, "news stories, then, become a forum for framing contests in which political actors compete in sponsoring their definitions of political issues" (Carragee, 1997, p. 2). Gamson, Crouteau, Hoynes and Sasson (1992) also express disapproval of framing practices in American media, arguing: "A media system suitable for a democracy ought to provide its readers with some coherent sense of the broader social forces that change the conditions of their everyday lives. It is difficult to find anyone who would claim that media discourse in the United States even remotely approaches this ideal" (p. 373).

Furthermore, despite an abundance of successful research that defines framing as an essential, universal aspect of news communication, some scholars equate framing with insincerity and manipulation. For instance, Parenti (1997) argues that players in the corporate media serve primarily corporate interests before attempting to inform the public of important knowledge and events (1997). Regarding framing, he asserts that the news media regularly fail to provide a range of information and commentary that might help citizens in a democracy develop their own critical perceptions. In response to this line of thinking, researchers have several answers. One belief is that framing is practical for sizing purposes. For example, Parenti (1997) writes that if time and space were limitless for news media, journalists could make a wider range of stories and information available to the public. The scholar suggests that critics should not condemn the media for restricting certain news items from reaching the headlines and airwaves. Furthermore, he asserts that one must accept framing as an essential function of news coverage because media organizations simply do not have the time, space, or tools to display all possible angles of every story that comes in. As a result, they must frame stories in a manner that is accessible and understood by the public.

The Pros and Cons of Frame Analysis

Precisely as framing in reporting is controversial, so is the field of frame analysis. Critics assert that such investigations are inherently subjective because the analyst comes to a lens with his or her ideology and understandings. Although there are useful tools for arriving at common or more accepted dominant readings, it is always possible that another reader will see an alternative. For this reason, such studies depend on the use of a sufficient number of examples to help readers decide for themselves if they agree with the researcher's line of reasoning when grouping items by frames.

While social scientists still debate the worth of this type of textual analysis, there is evidence that it is of value. For example, in his examination of television news coverage of Martin Luther King Day in his book Race, Myth and the News, Campbell (1995), pointed out that such research allows a reading of media texts in the context of larger cultural meanings. Similarly, Ragin (1992) pointed out the advantages of such analysis for social, historical, and cultural research in order to gather the context for the specific materials under study. Ragin also argued that this type of analysis is particularly appropriate when a researcher wishes to give a voice to a marginalized group in society, interpret historically or culturally significant phenomena, and advance theory.

For the present study, the researcher found that framing and gatekeeping analyses complement each other in looking at the dynamics at play in reference to black versus mainstream media's framing of racial profiling before and after September 11. Framing is particularly pertinent to this study because it usually occurs when one can present an issue using a variety of packages or thematic slants; the potential for framing the issue of racial profiling is present as with most public policy issues that are multidimensional (Nelson, Oxley & Clawson, 1997). Likewise, gatekeeper theory is useful because it allows the researcher to look at the dynamics at play with race and culture.

Combining Framing with Gatekeeping Theory

In addition to framers of the news, the media act as gatekeepers and interpreters. Gatekeeper theory is relevant to the study of black and general press coverage of the issue because race and culture play a key role in what is perceived as significant to reporters and editors. Gatekeepers at each newspaper type will have a different idea or perception of what is important and what they should cover in their respective news outlets. Assignment editors must approve events that reporters cover; furthermore, reporters must select the sources they will include in their article as well as the angle they will pursue, thus illustrating the gatekeeping theory.

In the end, journalists and editors draw maps or internal story patterns for their readers, and these maps or frames serve to outline public debate and influence readers' level of information (Gamson, 1992). According to Gamson (1992), the media act as gatekeepers and interpreters of political themes by selectively choosing to cover one or both sides of an issue, putting forth their own interpretation, or by allocating greater coverage to one issue over another (Gamson, 1992). These decisions directly change the media content that reaches audiences.

Researchers mainly apply traditional theories of gatekeeping to communication theory (Gieber, 1956; Shoemaker, 1991; White, 1950). These theories refer to gatekeeping as a selection process, offering communication scholars a framework for analyzing, evaluating, and comprehending how communication or news selection occurred and why journalists selected some items while rejecting others. Lewin (1947) introduced the term "gatekeeper" to the language in 1947, while White (1950) expanded the theory from the social psychology field to the communications field in 1950. Since then, researchers have used it frequently in studies of the mass communication process, especially in reference to any action that involved choosing or rejecting some potential items for publication.

White's study in 1950 found that editors play an important role in controlling what makes it past the gate and into the newspaper. In his study of news wires, White (1950) found that gatekeepers accepted or rejected articles based on built-in biases, experiences, attitudes, and expectations of the communication of news. In his model, stories are sent from gatekeeper to gatekeeper along the channels of communication, and choosing and discarding is a continuous process. White paid particular attention to editors' attitude toward certain news events, and to his or her personal prejudices and personal values in addition to his news judgment, noting the impact of time, parallel stories from different wires and space available.

The gatekeeper approach (Tuchman, 1978; Gans, 1979) is pertinent to the study of racial profiling because race and culture play a key role in what reporters and editors perceive as important. They must be somewhat subjective in their selection process to gather news that will appeal to their audience. Given media organizational routines, social movement actors must justify why some chronic problems such as poverty or racial injustice should receive more media attention today than other issues such as politics or education. In order to elevate routine issues onto media agendas, movement organizers must portray those issues as occurring or changing in exceptional fashion—increasing, spreading, and intensifying—so as to make them sufficiently interesting to warrant incorporation into media news gathering routines.

The gatekeeper process illustrates the fact that the gatekeeper's role is highly biased and based on his or her own set of experiences, attitudes, and expectations. White's model has served as the basis of subsequent research into the process of selection from news agency copy. Dimmick (1974) dubbed gatekeeping as an "uncertainty theory." He based this assumption on the idea that gatekeepers are uncertain about which events society will decide are news. He asserts that among factors contributing to selection process are opinion leaders, who themselves may be newsmakers; opinion leaders among journalists; reference groups within the newsroom; consensus of editorial staff; wire service budget recommendations; and timeliness. The researcher noted, however, that newspaper editors avoid the influence of television and radio newscasts. However, other evidence indicates that many newspaper gatekeepers often watch the evening newscasts and allow them to influence their judgment. Dimmick's model[4] also considers established policy, available space, and traditional news values. According to Dimmick, all of these factors may be responsible for the editor's decision to accept or reject an article.

While studying the flow of wire service news from the press associations to daily newspapers, Gieber (1956) expanded the White approach. Besides noting personal factors that influenced news judgment, he tried to measure the influence of wire services as well as other media. He found that the service the editor preferred and the one an individual reporter favored were important to the individual gatekeeper. Gieber also found that editors considered their most important task to provide their readers with what he called the top news of the day. In 1960, Gieber completed another gatekeeper study of five California newspapers. He analyzed the judgments and perceptions of those involved in transmitting news to the readers. He found that the accessibility of a source to newspapers is an important point. The source must decide whether the information is sufficiently important to his interest group and community. The reporter, on the other hand, must judge whether the information has some value according to his or her perception of news.

In other gatekeeper studies (Sigal, 1973; Gans, 1979), researchers generally focus on the conflict among gatekeepers and groups or individuals seeking to shape media content. Each step in the process presents a point where they choose to send the story, remove it, or to trim its content. Shoemaker and Reese (1996) found that factors such as news value, objectivity, and organizational structure serve as "checks and balances" on individual biases. These checks and balances may explain why news decisions across the media are often similar, despite the widely different personalities involved in making them (Riffe, Ellis, Rogers, Van Ommeren, & Woodman, 1986). Reese (2001) provides some basic questions we may ask when studying media content for frames: Whose principle was dominant in producing the observed coverage? How did the principles brought to bear by journalists interact with those promoted by their sources? These questions involve looking behind the scenes and making inferences from the symbolic patterns in news texts.

Further, in an overview of the concept and related research, Shoemaker (1991) extended the original model to take into account the wider social context and many factors at work. Shoemaker further stresses the importance of advertisers, public relations, pressure groups, and varied sources of news managers in influencing decisions. According to the researcher, gatekeeping usually involves multiple acts of gatekeeping over the period of news production, and group decision-making is often involved.

Criticisms of Gatekeeping Theory

Critics of gatekeeping theory often claim that its main weakness is the suggestion that there is only one main "gate area." For example, Bagdikian, in his RAND study (1973), speaks of the restraints on gatekeeping, focusing specifically on mechanical functions. His study touches on points salient to the concept of gatekeeping:

> Policy is exerted in effective ways. Editorial executives control assignment of stories, which is the most crucial decision in journalism. They decide whether a finished story will be used or not, and if used what emphasis and length. . . . Since newspaper staffs have a minimum of bureaucracy, tasks are carried out in an informal, highly personal atmosphere of professional camaraderie, so there is a tendency to avoid acrimony (p. 104).

Subsequent studies have indicated that the journalist's self-perception as the person who decides what people need to know is deeply ingrained. For instance, Whitney and Becker (1982) assert that media news editors choose their stories in proportion to the ratio in which they appear on the news service wires in a mixed pattern designed by wire service editors. The researchers hypothesize that wires offer a balanced menu each day, and news editor choices reflect the proportions in which they emerge on the wire. Because of the direct influence of the gatekeeper function, the researcher speculated that black and mainstream media would differ in how they frame and approach certain issues. The next section will explore their differences.

Studies note that the press prefers to present differences between the fortunes of whites and African Americans in terms of the high probability of black loss or in reference to bad news about blacks (Gandy, 1998). In addition, researchers have identified two striking regularities in points of view disseminated through media sources: crime is violent and criminal perpetrators are nonwhite (Entman, 1990; Gilliam, Iyengar, Simon & Wright, 1996). Entman (1990) notes that TV news, especially local news, paints a picture of blacks as violent and threatening toward whites, self-interested and demanding. An observable example took place on September 28, 2005, when conservative commentator, radio host, and former Reagan administration Secretary of Education Bill Bennett announced on his radio show, "Morning in America," "You could abort every black baby in this country, and your crime rate would go down." He followed up the comment with the idea that such a tactic would be an "impossible, ridiculous, morally reprehensible thing to do." But he insisted the strategy would work.

In terms of coverage of racial profiling and differences in how black press and mainstream media framed the issue, it is crucial to consider how newspapers cover marginalized groups in general. For example, Fedler (1973) found that minority groups received more attention than equivalent established groups in Minneapolis. However, stories about these unconventional groups often contained negative presentations. For example, Shoemaker (1984) found that deviant political groups, ranging from the NAACP to the Ku Klux Klan, receive less favorable coverage in major newspapers.

In surveys with news and political editors, she found that editors who perceive a group as deviant cover it less favorably because to present them favorably might go against the status quo. Baylor (1996) observed framing from the perspective of social movements, claiming they and the media are interdependent. In his content analysis of evening news segments from 1968 to 1979, Baylor (1996) identified five clear frames of American Indian protest coverage labeled as "militant," "stereotype," "treaty rights," "civil rights," and "factionalism." Scrutiny of these frames in action led Baylor to believe that "the very process of newsgathering and framing issues suggests that a distorted and incomplete picture of a movement's message" (p. 241).

Modern and Enlightened Racism

Other concepts that also help explain why media differences along color lines exist are modern racism and enlightened racism. Enlightened racism relies on the misunderstanding of the natural condition of most African Americans in the United States. For example, progressives who highlight positive images of African Americans, while ignoring serious problems faced by the black community, are guilty of "enlightened racism." Entman and Rojecki assert that the media have made great progress in portraying blacks; however, components of enlightened racism such as news coverage, television shows, advertising, and films, often inadvertently reinforce conventional hierarchies and stereotypes. Enlightened racism also creates the belief that anyone can succeed in the United States because of its fair system; therefore, it is the fault of the individual who does not succeed (Jhally & Lewis, 1992). Entman (1990) concludes that the presence of black anchors and authority figures on the news contributes to the characteristics of modern racism, or the belief that racial discrimination no longer exists in the United States. In addition, the press espouses tolerance but subtly perpetuates racist stereotyping by showing respect for black people's claims for justice but in the process framing them as a people who have or cause problems, or a "problem people" (Hartmann & Husband, 1974).

Although instances of overt racism in the media appear to be few, studies have shown that African-American and general press outlets handle stories differently. Fellows (1998) asserts that positive role models tend to differ among the two media types. Literature has affirmed the press represents African Americans in narrowly defined stereotypical roles (Corea, 1990; Diamond, 1991; MacDonald, 1992; Gutierrez, 1985). For instance, mainstream press tend to focus on mainstream entertainers and athletes such as Michael Jordan, Denzel Washington, or Ken Griffey Jr., while leaving out intellectual black role models such as former NASA astronauts Mae Jemison and Guion Blufords or members of Congress. Fellows (1998) said these differences make black-oriented newspapers valuable. Their editors have both a responsibility and an opportunity to tell the stories that their mainstream counterparts ignore.

Furthermore, studies throughout history have shown that mainstream and black press outlets have different ideas or perceptions of what is important and what they should cover in their respective newspapers. Examples of instances that the two types of newspapers covered issues differently include the Clarence Thomas confirmation hearings, the 1992 Los Angeles riots following the Rodney King verdict, and the O.J. Simpson murder trial (Dates & Barlow, 1993; Martindale, 1990). The Carl T. Rowan story is another example of how the two media outlets differ in their coverage (Dates & Barlow, 1993). In 1988, trespassers in his yard awakened the syndicated columnist and television-radio commentator. According to reports, Rowan, an advocate of gun control laws, called the police and, thinking they had arrived, opened a sliding door, only to see one of the intruders. The accounts of what transpired after that differ, but the intruder was shot in the wrist. The National Rifle Association and many people who opposed gun-control legislation, ridiculed Rowan.

The general press carried headlines such as "Columnist Shoots Teen Skinny Dipper" and "Rowan's Explanation of the Shooting was off Target." Further, the general press focused on the columns Rowan had written in strong favor of banning handguns. On the other hand, African-American press outlets looked at the same event from different perspectives (Dates & Barlow, 1993). Of the study's sample, 23 articles were neutral, coming from the general press and African-American publications. Five articles were positive, three of which were from the Washington Afro-American. Additionally, the national minority press organization, National Newspaper Publishers Association, passed a resolution in support of Rowan.

Fellows (1998) noted that welfare is another example of how the two media differ in their coverage of various issues.

> For years, employed blacks have been critical of the debilitating dependence on government aid that welfare has caused many in the black community to develop, sapping them of their motivation, ambition, and self-reliance. Yet the mainstream news outlets were so busy playing up the racial angle that they completely ignored this large segment of the black population. They also failed to make clear that the bulk of Californians on welfare happen to be white. The media bombard audiences with negative images of black men, whether it is convicted drug dealer "Freeway" Ricky Ross or slain rapper Tupac Shakur, Rodney King, or O.J. Simpson (p.10).

The Jake Powell incident provides yet another example of a difference in opinion in the two newspaper types. During a radio interview on July 29, 1938, New York Yankee outfielder Jake Powell said he worked as a police officer in the off-season and stayed in shape by cracking "niggers" over the head with his nightstick (Lamb, 1999). Officials suspended Powell immediately for ten days. Newspapers had different interpretations of what the event, and these interpretations varied usually according to the race of the journalist reporting the story. For instance, the New York Times characterized the comment as a flippant remark that was taken to be offensive to Chicago's black population. The Washington Post said that Powell had made an uncomplimentary remark about a portion of the population (Lamb, 1999). By comparison, it was a page-one story to black newspapers, which included more details, including reactions from the black community. The Chicago Defender reported that Elson asked, "How do you keep in trim during the winter months in order to keep up your batting average?" Powell then replied: "Oh, that's easy, I'm a policeman, and I beat niggers over the head with my blackjack" (Lamb, 1991, p. 21).

Lule (1995) uncovered similar findings in his study of how the media portrayed Mike Tyson during his rape trial. Lule noted that African-American writers brought a different point of view to the story, reflecting the idea that the African-American community sympathized with Tyson, while showing little sympathy for his accuser.

Research Questions and Rational

This study of how black and mainstream media covered racial profiling before and after September 11 uses content and textual analysis to examine the issue over a six-year period. Based on a review of the literature, five research questions guided this study of the issue as well as directed the development of the methodology for the result analyses. The questions were:

> RQ_1: How did black and mainstream newspapers differ in their location and types of articles printed about racial profiling before and after September 11?

RQ$_2$. How did black and mainstream newspapers differ in their use of frames in their coverage of the issue of racial profiling before and after September 11?

RQ$_3$. How did black and mainstream newspapers differ in their portrayal of racial and ethnic groups in their coverage of racial profiling before and after September 11?

RQ$_4$. How did black and mainstream newspapers differ in types of sources they used in their coverage of racial profiling before and after September 11?

RQ$_5$. How did black and mainstream newspapers differ in types of catchphrases they used in their coverage of racial profiling before and after September 11?

Rationale

Journalists play the vital role of defining and placing on paper the meanings of events for their audience, and theoretically, September 11 should influence how they framed the issue of racial profiling because of the nature of the tragic event. Without a doubt, the terrorist attacks created an environment in which most Americans were equally threatened. In addition to the demographics of journalists, the mission of a newspaper obviously has an impact on how it frames certain issues.

History has shown that gatekeepers at mainstream and black press outlets have different ideas or perceptions of what is important and what journalists should cover in their respective news outlets. African-American and mainstream newspapers are aimed at different populations; therefore, one might speculate they would contain different frames. Mainstream newspapers target a general audience, while black press newspapers speak to the issues of interest to African-American readers (Dates & Barlow, 1993).

Within the framing body of work, history has shown that socioeconomic status, race, and education can make a difference in how reporters frame certain issues. This is of significance, according to Gans (1979), because the majority of journalists come from an upper-middle to upper-class background, which he asserts is a distinctly white perspective. Van Dijk (1993) adds that, ''News is largely produced by white journalists who have grown up with a set of dominant white group norms and values, which tend to define an overall white perspective on news events'' (p. 245). On the other hand, historically, the African-American press has challenged racial injustice, preserved, and highlighted African-American culture and heritage. This advocacy role has directed the African-American press to focus on interpreting and reframing news more often than reporting timely or news-breaking events (Wolseley, 1990).

A look at sources is important because frames manifest themselves in a reporter's selection of sources. In fact, reporters may use sources effectively as framing devices by creating the illusion of validity or factuality, or by adding credibility to certain points of view (Pan & Kosicki, 1993). Reporters can add weight to a point of view by quoting official sources or marginalize certain viewpoints by relating a quote to a social deviant. The positions of power of these sources will determine how readers or viewers interpret the content that is presented or left out in black and mainstream media. Reporters use quotes from certain sources with race, points of view, and values in mind to add or take away credibility from certain viewpoints. Therefore, quotes can serve to amplify the framing choices journalists make while constructing the news. Furthermore, a frame analysis is relevant because a difference in frames almost always exists when issues are multidimensional. For example, the Million Man March can be presented as a disruption of political order or as an exercise in free speech (Nelson, Oxley & Clawson, 1997).

Finally, the researcher analyzed catchphrases because frames often manifest themselves in a reporter's selection of certain definitions and catchphrases consciously or subconsciously. Catchphrases are defined as provocative words or phrases to describe situations or individuals. This can also be an indication of the types of frames that reporters use in their coverage of the topic.

Chapter Four: Methodology

Using a content and textual analysis, the researcher looked at both editorial and hard news stories published in five black press and five general press newspapers three years before and three years after September 11. Content analysis is a widely accepted practice in communications research to determine news media frames (Entman, 1990). The basic technique is to capture news reports—either broadcast or print—over a given time period and code them for a particular issue.

Furthermore, the researcher used the core principles of strategic frame analysis to ascertain major frames that characterize reporting on the issue of racial profiling, as well as an understanding of what the media chooses to ignore. Overall, this approach allows researchers to identify the relevant news media frames. The study includes reading and identification of the key words and themes emphasized in the selected articles (Entman, 1991).

To determine inter-coder reliability for one dominant frame in each article, the researcher used Cronbach's alpha, which measures how well a set of variables measures a single construct and reliability or consistency. The researcher used this measure to assess the relationship between the categories assigned by two students who coded the same articles to determine if the dependent measure was reliable (or at least around .70).

The study used the same code sheet for all coders and included a codebook to operationalize definitions that might not be clear. A coder reliability assessment was conducted with a random sample of 10 percent of the total stories coded, or 70 stories total. The researcher then assessed the coding for each of the frames for percentage of agreement. When the coding scheme had more than eighteen subcategories, Cronbach's alpha revealed that the measure of relationship closeness was not reliable, $\alpha = .64$. But when the coding was collapsed into seven categories, Cronbach's alpha revealed that the measure of relationship closeness was reliable, $\alpha = .74$. The researcher coded more than 80 percent of the articles.

Coding Scheme

The coding scheme consists of five sections. The first section deals with details such as location, length, newspaper, and type of story, whether straight news or editorial. The second section looks at the news sources, which were: citizen, law enforcer, political leader, agency, or institution representative, professor, poll/study, clergy, and victim or victim's family. The race of sources was not coded because the researcher found it too difficult to determine a source's ethnicity based on the context of the article. In most instances, the person's race or religion was not mention at all.

The third section looks at the ethnic group covered in each article. Categories are: Arab/Middle Easterner, African Americans, Hispanics, and other multiple groups. Coders checked these categories only if reporters mentioned the victim's race in the article. If the article mentioned more than one race, coders selected multiple groups. If it did not mention race, coders left it blank.

In the fifth section, the variable consisted of the following categories, which were thought to suggest the frames listed below. Each article was assigned to the most prominent frame in the story. Frames were:

1. The repeating history/slave frame focuses on how reporters compare racial profiling to other historical events such as concentration camps and internment camps, in which large groups of people were targeted because of their ethnicity. For example, slave-framed articles might include a comparison of racial profiling articles to the mistreatment of slaves that took place during the slave era. The threat to civil liberties frame depicts racial profiling as a threat to the basic rights of individuals.
2. The urban myth/necessary evil frame explores whether racial profiling really exists. It also describes racial profiling as a sensible tactic that police officers use to catch criminals.
3. The financial/litigation frame looks at the expenses surrounding racial profiling incidents, including civil suits, court cases, ongoing investigations, and fees for public relations and how these expenses might transfer to citizens through taxes, etc.
4. Legislation/prevention/reform-oriented frames focuses on measures taken to decrease cases of racial profiling. Articles also focused on

local laws connected to racial profiling as well as bills introduced to legislatures to ban racial profiling.

5. The human-interest frame describes the plight of the victims of racial profiling and specific incidents during which racial profiling took place.

6. The protest/rally frame deals with citizen-initiated efforts to curb racial profiling.

7. Other: Articles that did not fit into the other categories were placed in other.

Note: The researcher opted not to include a terrorism or violence frame because an argument could have been made for most articles to fall into such a category after September 11.

Sample

The African-American newspapers in the sample were the Chicago Defender, Washington Informer, the Philadelphia Tribune, the Atlanta Inquirer, and the New York Beacon. The researcher selected these newspapers because they are located in cities with large African-American populations, and they have had many high-profile cases of racial profiling (see section below). According to the 2000 Census, the ten states with the largest black populations in 2000 were New York, California, Texas, Florida, Georgia, Illinois, North Carolina, Maryland, Michigan, and Louisiana (McKinnon, 2000). Furthermore, of all places in the United States with populations of 100,000 or more, New York had the largest black population with 2.3 million, followed by Chicago (1.1 million). Detroit, Philadelphia, and Houston had black populations between 500,000 and 1 million. The cities also contain some of the more notable black newspapers. For example, the Philadelphia Tribune is the nation's oldest continuously published black newspaper. The Chicago Defender is one of the only African American dailies in the country and one of the most historically influential. In addition, these publications included a good selection of articles that focused on racial profiling during the period under inspection.

The researcher matched these publications with mainstream newspapers located in the same cities. Consequently, the general press newspapers were the Chicago Sun-Times, Washington Post, Philadelphia Enquirer, the Atlanta Journal & Constitution, and the New York Daily News. These mainstream publications are weeklies or dailies with substantial circulation in large metropolitan areas. They often have resources concentrated on their local/regional desks and may use wire service stories to supplement their coverage.

The researcher accessed the articles using Lexis Nexis and Ethnic News, a full-text source for minority newspapers. The key words used for the search were "racial profiling," which were adequate to produce enough articles for this study. The researcher included ethnic profiling as a key word in the pilot study; however, it did not return a significant number of hits.

Background of Research Cities

In order to understand the frames used to cover racial profiling in the research cities, one must know the background of each one. This section looks at some of the notable racial profiling cases in each city as well as legislation and reform tactics used to end racial profiling in each one. It also offers a detailed description of the newspapers used in this study's sample.

As often noted in the literature, the racial profiling of blacks and Hispanics grew out of the war on drugs (Harris, 1999), which President Ronald Reagan kicked off in 1982 with the establishment of a task force to increase air and sea operations against drug smuggling in the South Florida area. In an effort to combat and eliminate the lucrative businesses dealers had established in the inner cities during the 1980s, many government officials initiated major law enforcement programs to deal with street-level drug dealing. The operations targeted poor, minority, urban neighborhoods where drug dealing tended to be open and easy to detect (Harris, 1999). The goal of these inner-city efforts was to make as many arrests as possible. The plan worked. Arrests for drug possession reported by state and local police nearly doubled nationwide from 400,000 in 1981 to 762,718 in 1988. Comparable figures for arrests for drug sale and manufacture rose from 150,000 in 1981 to 287,858 in 1988. However, the downside to this success was the disproportionately representation of minorities in these figures (Harris, 1999).

Racial Profiling in the Windy City

Each city in the sample has had its share of racial profiling reports; however, Chicago was perhaps the most intriguing. Data analysis from Northwestern University's Center for Public Safety has shown that Chicago police made more than 244,000 traffic stops in 2004. Of that number, more than half of the drivers stopped were minorities. Police stopped African American drivers at a rate 27 percent higher than the estimated African American population in Chicago. Although, police stopped minority drivers more frequently, they still were more willing to have their cars searched than their white counterparts.

The Chicago Sun provides an example of the treatment of racial profiling victims in a June 28, 2000, article:

> By the time he turned 24, Hoffman Estates police because of his race had harassed Logan Smith many times about his rare birth defect, his family claims. The family's lawsuit alleged that Smith was targeted by police because he was African-American and because police knew he had no genitalia because of surgeries to correct a birth defect and had been raised as a girl (p.3).

Also in Chicago, victims reported 55 hate crimes post September 11. Examples included an incident in which an angry mob descended on a mosque and the beating of Chicago-area taxi driver. To crack down on the cases of racial profiling in the city, the City Council passed ordinances prohibiting racial profiling by the Chicago Police Department, or any other law enforcement agency operating within the city limits. The proposal addressed concerns over civil rights violations raised by numerous cases of alleged racial profiling uncovered across the United States.

Both the Chicago Defender and the Chicago Sun-Times are notable publications that provided depth to the study. Founded in 1905 by Robert Sengstacke Abbott, the Chicago Defender has been the voice of the African-American community in Chicago and across the United States for 100 years. The newspaper has covered such topics as lynchings, racism, and segregation.

According to Lexis Nexis, The Chicago Sun-Times is a major Midwestern newspaper that provides extensive coverage of news, business, political, and social issues in addition to local and regional events of Chicago's metropolitan area. The Chicago Sun-Times is one of the 10 largest daily newspapers in the United States. The publication has won eight Pulitzer Prizes.

Profiling in Philadelphia

Philadelphia has also had its share of racial profiling incidents. In a study of its 23 police districts, the American Civil Liberties Union found that police stopped blacks a great deal more often than they stopped whites. Blacks make up 42 percent of Philadelphia's population, based on 1995 Census data, but accounted for 60 percent of all stops. Whites, who make up 54 percent of the population, accounted for only 36 percent, the report said. Further, police stopped 36 percent of all minorities without legal justification. The American Civil Liberties Union and NAACP have monitored the Philadelphia police since 1996, when the city settled a federal lawsuit in the wake of a police corruption scandal (Ramasastry, 2002.)

Interesting cases in the city include the shooting death of Timothy Thomas and the civil unrest that followed. On April 7, 2001, police shot the unarmed citizen and Cincinnati residents responded with more than a week of protest. In another incident, air marshals handcuffed and detained a 54-year-old Florida doctor of Indian descent because they did not like the way he looked. In letters sent to lawmakers in Philadelphia and Florida, American Civil Liberties Union officials described how the doctor became a victim of racial profiling after a flight on which air marshals subdued an unruly passenger and held other passengers at gunpoint for 30 minutes (Ramasastry, 2002).

The city is home to The Philadelphia Tribune, America's oldest newspaper and the Greater Philadelphia region's largest daily newspaper dedicated to serving the African-American community. Publishers founded the Tribune more than 120 years ago to provide information on diverse issues and events on the local, national, and international level. The Philadelphia Daily News is a general circulation newspaper providing local and some national news coverage. It offers reporting on politics, industry, crime, crime prevention, education, banking, and transportation. Publishers founded the Philadelphia Daily News on March 31, 1925, and Knight Newspapers, Inc. acquired it, along with The Philadelphia Inquirer, in 1969. The paper covers local news and sports. It has a reputation for a willingness to be unorthodox.

Washington, D.C.'s Racial Profiling Woes

Washington, D.C., has also had its share of racial profiling troubles. In fact, in March 2001, the Metropolitan Police Department admitted that its officers had exchanged e-mails about one another and citizens containing racist, sexist, and homophobic language. The announcement raised concerns about police bias and racial profiling. As a result, in late March 2001, MPD Chief Charles H. Ramsey pledged that his department would collect information on traffic stops.[i] With the Racial Profiling Prohibition Act of 2001, the legislation sought to prohibit racial profiling and to ensure that law enforcement agencies no longer detain people on the street because of their skin color, nationality, or ethnicity. The law also sought to eliminate legal and constitutional problems that arise when police stop a person.

The Washington Informer is a weekly that publishers contend only covers positive news. It reaches more than 50,000 readers serving the District of Columbia, Prince George's County, Montgomery County, and Northern Virginia. According to its Web site, its distribution is 15,000 to newsstands, and 750 to subscribers. The Washington Post, founded in 1877, specializes in in-depth news, analysis of American politics and insightful coverage of national and international trends and events. The Washington Post Company is a diversified media and education company whose principal operations include newspaper and magazine publishing, television broadcasting, cable television systems, electronic information services, and educational and career services.

Atlanta's Troubles

With its large minority population, it is not surprising that Atlanta has had a number of racial profiling incidents. Many complaints focused on the city's airport where victims reported that airport law enforcers sought African American women and other minorities for contraband at much higher rates than they searched other segments of the population traveling internationally, even though the women targeted were statistically less likely than other passengers to carry contraband. For example, Cathy Harris, a whistleblower, reported that racial profiling took place regularly in the U.S. Customs Department at Atlanta's Hartsfield Airport where she worked as a senior inspector. Ultimately, her superiors harassed and intimidated her, and eventually suspended her without pay. Administrators allowed Harris to return to work in the winter of 2000, but her employers did not reinstate her until January 2001.

To help curb the number of racial profiling incidents in Atlanta, the Georgia House of Representative passed legislation in 2004, which forbids any law enforcement employee to use a person's race or ethnicity as the sole purpose for establishing probable cause to stop a vehicle. Secondly, it requires state and local law enforcement agencies to hold annual training sessions that instruct law enforcement personnel on policies against racial profiling. The bill also requires law enforcement personnel to maintain a record of each of their vehicles, which would include the person's gender, race, suspected violation, etc. The law enforcement agency is to maintain this data by for at least seven years (Daily Report, 2004).

Publishers founded the Atlanta Journal & Constitution more than 120 years ago. The newspaper has a daily circulation of 450,000 and 650,000 on Sunday, according to its Web site. The paper covers topics such as business, finance, transportation, industry, and trade. It includes staff-generated news, features, business, sports, and editorials. The newspaper also contains local news, which includes coverage of Hartsfield International Airport, where victims report many racial profiling incidents. According to Lexis Nexis, the Atlanta Inquirer has a readership of more than 200,000 in the Atlanta area; and readers are predominantly educated, informed, affluent African-American consumers.

Troubles in the Big Apple

New York has had some of the most publicized racial profiling cases. In this city, the issue has been controversial. Due in part to an incident in New York, the term "racial profiling" became even more popular in 1998 when two white New Jersey state troopers pulled over a van for speeding. As they approached the van from behind, it suddenly reversed toward them. The troopers fired eleven shots from their handguns, wounding three of the van's four occupants, who were all black or Hispanic.

High profile civil suits in the city have been numerous. For example, the courts settled a class-action lawsuit that alleged police officers used racial profiling in 2003. Plaintiffs filed the lawsuit in 1999 because police officers had unjustly stopped and searched them. Under terms of the settlement, city officials asked the police department to document instances when it stops and frisks people and will better train its officers to carry out those duties. The city also agreed to pay $167,500 in damages to ten plaintiffs.

Perhaps the biggest scandal in the city occurred when the city's police department faced allegations of police misconduct for the shooting of Amadou Diallo. In February 1999, four New York City police officers searching for a rape suspect knocked on Amadou Diallo's door to question him. When he came to the door he reached inside his jacket, at which point, officers shot at him forty-one times, hitting him with nineteen bullets. Diallo was reaching for what turned out to be his wallet. The torture of Abner Louima is another high profile case. New York police officers sodomized the New York City resident with a plunger handle while he was inside a precinct office. The incident reinforced already-existing perceptions that the NYPD uses excessive force.

To help end racial profiling in New York, Police Commissioner Raymond Kelly barred racial profiling in a March 2002 order. Further, a bill negotiated by the City Council and Mayor Bloomberg instituted Kelly's ban, which prohibits police officers as well as other law enforcement agents employed by the city from using race, ethnicity, religion, or national origin as the determinate factor for law enforcement actions. Prior to these efforts, in 2001, the Justice Department mandated reforms for the New Jersey Highway Patrol, including training on stopping, searching, and seizing. The department imposed new requirements on data collection and installed video cameras in every single patrol car (Elder, 2001).

New York newspapers also frequently focused on the New Jersey Turnpike, which is nicknamed "White Man's Pass." According to reports, the New Jersey Highway Patrol considers the turnpike a popular route for drug traffickers.

Officers, however, stop a disproportionately high number of minorities. And, in 1998, New Jersey officers shot and wounded three black motorists, which encouraged officials to launch an investigation into allegations of racial profiling (Elder, 2001).

The New York Daily News is New York City's highest-circulated tabloid and the fifth largest newspaper in the country, according to its Web site. Known as New York's hometown paper, the News focuses its coverage on what is happening in the boroughs of the city and New York. Publishers founded the New York Beacon more than 20 years ago to highlight people and events not traditionally featured in general market newspapers. It caters to the city's large African-American and Caribbean community.

Chapter Five: Findings

The research questions emphasized comparisons between black and mainstream newspaper coverage of racial profiling over time. To measure this difference, the researcher looked at both quantitative and qualitative changes in the media before and after September 11. This section explores the quantitative portion of the study. To assess the percentage of articles about racial profiling published before and after the tragedy, the researcher looked at Table 1, which shows that both black and mainstream media generated about the same number of articles pre- and post-September 11. However, the number of articles printed before the tragedy, 384, was slightly higher than the 323 articles printed after the event.

Within the black press category, the Philadelphia Daily printed the most articles about racial profiling before the event, while the Chicago Defender printed the most stories after September 11. In mainstream media, the Atlanta Journal Constitution printed the most articles about the issue before the event, while the Washington Post printed the most articles about the issue after the event (Table 1).

Furthermore, the significant quantity of articles published about this theme both before and after September 11 suggests that editors and reporters viewed the issue as an important and newsworthy topic. The span of three years before and three years after provided a sufficient sample for analysis.

TABLE 1
Frequencies for numbers of articles in each publication mentioning racial profiling before and after September 11.

Publication Title	Pre	Post
Black		
Washington Informer	24	14
New York Beacon	26	33
Philadelphia Daily	70	27
Chicago Defender	60	39
Atlanta Inquirer	13	7
Mainstream		
Philadelphia Tribune	33	11
Washington Post	41	98
New York Daily News	54	20
Chicago Sun	2	21
Atlanta Journal Constitution	63	53
Total	386	323

Location of Articles

The next section looked at emphasis or location of articles about racial profiling. The essence of framing according to Entman (1991) is sizing, or to what extent is any depicted reality magnified or miniaturized and thus made more or less significant. Therefore, the first research question asked:

RQ$_1$: How did black and mainstream newspapers differ in their location and types of articles printed about racial profiling before and after September 11?

TABLE 2
Percentage of articles focusing on racial profiling on page one of black
and mainstream newspapers.

	Pre	Post
Black Press Page One Inside	19% 81	8% 92
	100% (N= 156)	100% (N=131)
Mainstream Page One Inside	13% 87	12% 87

100% (N=217)   100% (N=185)
X^2=0.1015 X^2=0.1015
P=0.5653   p=0.2141

Table 2 shows that September 11 and publication type did not make a significant difference in placement of articles about racial profiling (p>.05). Most articles about racial profiling for both black and mainstream media fell inside the newspaper. Secondly, date did not make a difference. For both before and after September 11, editors placed most articles about racial profiling inside the newspaper. Before September 11, black press published 19 percent of its articles on page one, while it published 8 percent on page one after the tragedy. On the other hand, 13 percent of mainstream media articles about racial profiling were on page one before September 11; while 12 percent fell on page one after the event.

Types of Articles: News Vs. Editorial

To assess the emphasis of racial profiling articles by black and mainstream media, the researcher looked at percentages of editorials and straight news articles about the topic. Table 3 shows there is a significant difference in types of articles based on publication type before and after September 11 (p<.05). Several conclusions are worth noting. First, the researcher found that both before and after September 11, black and mainstream newspapers were more likely to run straight news stories rather than editorials about racial profiling. Before the tragedy, 75 percent of black press articles about racial profiling were hard news-based, while after the tragedy, 68 percent were news-based. Similarly, for mainstream media 88 percent of articles about racial profiling were news-based before September 11, while 74 percent were news-based after the event.

TABLE 3
Percentage of editorials and hard news articles focusing on racial profiling in black and mainstream newspapers.

Publication Type	Pre	Post
Black Hard News Editorials	75% 25	68% 31
	100% (N=156)	100%(N=131)
Mainstream Hard News Editorials	88% 12	74% 26
	100% (N=228) x^2=10.136 p=0.0015	100% (N=192) x^2=2.264 p=0.3225

TABLE 4
Percentage of articles focusing on racial profiling with bylines versus wire in black and mainstream newspapers before and after September 11.

	Pre	Post
Black Bylines	75%	60%
Wire or no name	25	40
	100% (N= 154)	100% (N=131)
Mainstream Bylines	61%	70%
Wire or no name	39	30
	100% (N= 230)	100% (N=192)
	x^2=29.028	X^2=13.874
	p<0.0001	p<0.0031

Newspaper Vs. Wire

Table 4 suggests several findings, including how the two newspaper types differed significantly (p<.05) in their use of local versus wire services both before and after September 11, 2001. Most of the articles for both black press and mainstream media were local in nature. In fact, prior to the tragedy, 25 percent of articles in black press newspapers were from a wire service or did not include a byline. On the other hand, 40 percent of mainstream articles about racial profiling did not have a byline. After the event, wire stories increased in black publications to 40 percent, while the number decreased in mainstream publications to 30 percent.

Media Portrayals of Ethnic Groups

The next set of analyses examined how the two media types portrayed ethnic groups in their coverage. The researcher speculated that the newspaper types would differ in the sorts of groups they focused on in their coverage of racial profiling. The research question was:

RQ$_3$. How did black and mainstream newspapers differ in their portrayal of racial and ethnic groups in their coverage of racial profiling; what influence did September 11 have?

Table 5 shows that the two newspaper types differed significantly both before and after September 11 (p<.05) in the ethnic groups they covered. Prior to September 11, both black and mainstream newspapers tended to focus their attention on African Americans, which made up 65 percent of black press articles and 57 percent of mainstream media articles. The second most popular category for both media was multiple groups, which made up 33 percent of black press and 40 percent mainstream media articles.

However, after September 11, the two newspaper types differed in the ethnic groups they covered. Mainstream media shifted its focus to Arabs/Middle Easterners, which made up 51 percent of the sample, while black press newspapers continued to focus predominantly on African Americans, which made up 49 percent of its sample. The second most popular category for black press and mainstream media was multiple groups, which made up 39 percent of black press articles and 49 percent of mainstream articles after the tragedy.

TABLE 5

Percentage of ethnic groups covered in black and mainstream hard news articles about racial profiling before and after September 11.

	Pre	Post
Black Newspapers		
Arab/Middle Easterner	1%	11%
Black	65	49
Asian	1	1
Multiple Groups	33	39
	100% (N=129)	100% (N=107)
Mainstream Newspapers		
Arab/Middle Easterner	0%	51%
Black	57	18
Asian	3	2
Multiple Groups	40	29
	100% (N=164)*	100% (N=175)*
	$X^2=73.314$	$x^2=73.314$
	P=.00001	p=.00001

*some articles did not mention a race.

Newspaper Source Selection

The subsequent set of analyses examined the relationship between news sources and the newspaper type, before and after September 11. The question was:

RQ$_4$. How did black and mainstream newspapers differ in types of sources they used in their coverage of racial profiling before and after September 11?

Table 6 shows several results that are worth mentioning. First, there was a significant difference in the types of sources black and mainstream media selected in their coverage of racial profiling ($p<.05$). Secondly, findings showed pre-September 11, the most common source for black press was civil rights agency representative, which made up 21 percent, while the most popular source quoted by mainstream media was law enforcer, which made up 28 percent.

TABLE 6
Percentage of sources used in black and mainstream hard news articles about racial profiling before and after September 11.

	Pre	Post		Pre	Post
Black			**Mainstream**		
1. Citizen	3%	10%		8%	30%
2. Law enforcer, police officer	17	12		28	21
3. Clergy, i.e. minister	15	5		7	2
4. Politician, i.e. mayor	13	16		22	14
5. Activist, i.e. Jesse Jackson	11	5		7	5
6. Civil rights representative	21	26		5	10
7. Victim or victim's family	8	8		5	10
8. Attorney/judge	6	9		9	3
9. Legislator	4	8		7	1
12. Study/ Poll	2	0		2	1
13. other	0	1		0	3
	100% (N=123)	100% (N=96)		100% (N=199)	100% (N=140)
	x^2=42.911	x^2=42.533		x^2=42.911	x^2=42.533
	p=0.0001	p=0.0001		P=0.0001	p=0.0001

*Based on total number of sources in hard news articles.

Thirdly, the second most popular source for black press was law enforcer, which made up 17 percent of its sources, while the second most popular source for mainstream media was politician, which made up 16 percent of its sources. Post-September 11, the most popular category for black press remained civil right's representatives, which made up 26 percent of its sources, while the most popular category for mainstream media was citizen, which made up 30 percent of its sources. The second most popular source for black press was politician, at 16 percent, while for mainstream media it was law enforcer, at 21 percent.

Catchphrases for Racial Profiling

Frames manifest themselves in a reporter's selection of sources as well as the use of certain definitions, catchphrases, etc. that reporters consciously or subconsciously select for articles. The definition of catchphrase is the recurring use of provocative words or phrases to describe situations or individuals. The research question for this section was:

RQ$_5$. How did black and mainstream newspapers differ in types of catchphrases they used in their coverage of racial profiling before and after September 11?

The most notable finding from Table 7 is that reporters did not use catchphrases much in articles focusing on racial profiling. Only 45 total articles included a catchphrase. Furthermore, there was not a significant difference in the catchphrases black and mainstream media used to frame racial profiling before September 11. However, after the event, there was a significant difference (p>.05).

Prior to September 11, the most popular catchphrase for both groups was "Driving While Black." For the black press, the frame made up 71 percent of its articles about racial profiling; while for mainstream media, the frame made up 87 percent of its articles about racial profiling. The second most popular catchphrase before September 11 for black press was "Flying While Black," which made up 30 percent of its articles about the issue; while it was "Flying While Black" for mainstream media at 13 percent of its articles.

TABLE 7

Percentage of articles using catchphrases in black and mainstream articles about racial profiling before and after September 11.

	Pre	Post
Black		
Driving While Black	71%	85%
Flying While Arab	0	0
Flying While Black	30	15
	100% (N=17)	100% (N=13)
Mainstream		
Driving While Black	87%	44%
Flying While Arab	0	28
Flying While Black	13	28
	100% (N=8)	100% (N=7)
	x^2=3.563	x^2=5.804
	p=0.1684	p=0.054

Post-September 11, the most popular catchphrase for both groups was "Driving While Black" at 85 percent for the black press, and 44 percent for the mainstream media. The second most popular catchphrase for black press after the tragedy was "Flying While Black" at 15 percent; while for mainstream media, it was "other" and "Flying While Arab," at 28 percent each.

Reporters used the most common catchphrase, "Driving While Black" in their respective publications to frame racial profiling as a nagging threat that many minorities often endure. The following use of the catchphrase appeared in the Chicago Defender February 21, 2000, issue: "Scores of African Americans—including athletes, members of Congress, actors, business leaders—have experienced the humiliation of being stopped on the nation's roads for no other reason than the alleged traffic offense derisively referred to as 'Driving While Black,' (DWB)?" (Ruklick, 2000, p.1)

On Aug. 6, 2000, The Sun featured an article that focused on how a mostly white, affluent North Shore suburb could be a role model for other communities. It stated that rather than following the lead of less-progressive communities and denying accusations that people were stopped for "Driving While Black" or questioned as criminal suspects because of their color or religion. Instead, its City Council voted to look deeper into the charges, which surfaced in a federal lawsuit, filed by five current or former police officers (Ruffins, 2000, p. 12).

The catchphrase mutated after the first phase and other terms emerged, including "Flying While Black." A Chicago Defender April 11, 2000, article focused on how African Americans are more likely to be stripped searched and x-rayed even though they are less likely to be found carrying illegal drugs through airports. The article stated that "Durbin was determined to end the 'Flying While Black' syndrome that has caused scores of black women to be stopped and body searched by U.S. Customs inspectors who, because of racial profiling, detained more African American women than any others" (Stausberg, 2000, p. 4).

Interestingly, some of the catchphrases reporters and editors created in the media to cover racial profiling have become permanent fixtures in the English vernacular. Catchphrases such as DWB are successful because they play off other familiar terms that have been around for decades such as "Driving under the Influence" (DUI) or "Driving While Intoxicated" (DWI).

How the Frames Stacked Up

The bulk of this analysis focuses on how black and mainstream media framed the issue of racial profiling. The study began with the expectation that black and mainstream newspapers would frame the issue differently based on demographics served and missions. Presumably, September 11 would have an influence on these differences because of the horrendous nature of the event. To assess these differences, if any, the researcher used a qualitative analysis for this portion of the study. This section explores the different types of frames in more detail and looks at some specific examples. In frame analysis, examples often provide insight into the types of frames that researchers uncovered. The research question for this section was:

RQ$_2$. How did black and mainstream newspapers differ in the use of frames in their coverage of the issue of racial profiling before and after September 11?

Table 8 shows a significant difference (p>.05) in the framing of racial profiling both before and after September 11, 2001. Several findings are worth noting. First, the most common frame before and after September 11 for both black and mainstream press was legislation, which made up 43 percent and 26 percent of black press articles before and after September 11 and 43 and 29 percent of articles for mainstream media before and after September 11.

Legislation and reform frames for both black and mainstream newspapers usually focused on current bills under consideration by state legislatures. For example, The Washington Post on June 18, 2003, published an article about President George Bush issuing the first broad ban against racial profiling by federal law enforcement agencies. Another example of the legislation frame included in the Washington Post on January 12, 2002, which discussed a bill the Virginia governor introduced to prohibit racial profiling

TABLE 8

Percentages of articles with racial profiling frames in black and mainstream media before and after September 11.

	Pre	Post		Pre	Post
Black			**Mainstream**		
History/slave	5%	7%		0%	2%
Dream/protest/rally	8	4		1	1
Threat to civil liberties	11	15		6	10
Urban myth/racial profiling necessary evil	0	0		1	1
Financial	1	0		4	2
Litigation	10	25		18	12
Legislation /prevention	43	26		43	29
Human interest's story	1	1		0	1
Poll/study	1	3		2	11
Protest	12	9		14	19
Campaign	4	3		11	6
Other	6	7		1	7
	100% (N=154)	100% (N=127)		100% (N=228)	100% (N=191)
	x^2=40.869 p=0.0001	x^2=54.190 p=0.0001		x^2=40.869 p=0.0001	x^2=54.190 p=0.0001

and to ensure that law enforcement agencies stopped detaining people on the street because of their skin color, nationality, or ethnicity (Melton, 2002).

Findings indicate that the second most common frame before September 11 for black press media was protest, which made up 12 percent of its articles, while the second most popular frame for mainstream media during this period was financial/litigation, which made up 10 percent of its articles. Perhaps in response to the impact news value, reporters, and editors might use the financial/litigation frame to help their readers perceive the issue as more important. Coverage of this issue using this frame was two-pronged—some articles focused on lawsuits, while others focused on the coverage of cities' expenses incurred in dealing with racial profiling. Articles containing this frame dealt with the operating costs of investigations, litigation, and peripheral expenses such as public relations and taxes, etc.

An example of the financial theme was in The Chicago Sun March 8, 2000, issue, which discussed the money one Chicago suburb paid litigants after a racial profiling case (Guerrero, 2000). It stated: "Mount Prospect is likely to end up paying $400,000 in legal fees to attorneys who represented the village and its police department against the three federal lawsuits that were settled" (p. 6). Additionally, other articles expressed outrage at the amount of money the city paid a PR firm to help improve its image following allegations of racial profiling. For example, a March 9, 2000, article stated that Highland Park had hired a public relations firm after five police officers filed a federal lawsuit accusing the department's top brass of encouraging officers to pull over black or Hispanic drivers (Guerrero, 2000).

Protest/Meeting

The protest frame focused on events organized to stress the evils of racial profiling. Activists often orchestrated rallies in response to specific incidents. For example, a Philadelphia Tribune June 5, 2001, article described the actions of a group of twenty-five to thirty activists who gathered with picket signs and bullhorns in an attempt to let people know there was a "growing movement" across the country against police brutality, racial profiling, and racial bias in the criminal justice system. The article also detailed how protestors showed their support and solidarity for activists in Cincinnati after the shooting death of an African American. Moreover, the Associated Press reported the aftermath of what happened when a Muscogee County grand jury decided not to indict a former sheriff's deputy for the fatal shooting of a man who was killed during a traffic stop connected to a drug investigation. To bolster support, activist Jesse Jackson held a protest against police brutality and to help the family of the victim (Associated Press, 2004).

A large portion of articles containing the protest frame also focused on the 2000 Redeem the Dream Rally orchestrated by the late Dr. Martin Luther King's son, Martin Luther King III, and his mother, Coretta Scott King. For example, an August 29, 2000, article states that Dr. King's dream for many blacks had turned into a virtual nightmare. The article adds that about 100,000 demonstrators called on America to live up to its principles of life, liberty, and the pursuit of happiness described in the Constitution. Furthermore, a June 6, 2000, article stressed the importance of "redeeming the dream." In the article, Dr. Martin Luther King's son said: "It is time to 'Redeem the Dream' and awaken the American consciousness to the reality of racial profiling" (p. 1).

Another example of the frame is found in this January 13, 2000, article in which activist Jesse Jackson states that confederates undercut the American dream, and so dreamers must not let dream-busters destroy America's hope (Strausberg, 2000, p. 1). "All white folks are not racist, [Jesse L. Jackson Sr.] told a cheering audience at Dr. King's Workshop, 930 E. 50th St. They assumed because they had white skin that they were as immoral as they were, but they said, 'No, we're white but we also want to be morally right.'" (p. 1)

Further, a June 6, 2000, article stressed the importance of ending racial profiling. It stated that Dr. King's son, and national activists made plans to repeat the historic 1963 March on Washington. In addition, King said: "It is time to 'Redeem the Dream' and awaken the American consciousness to the reality of racial profiling." Ruklick (2000) included this except:

Bigotry took on a new face here during recent months as charges of racial profiling swept the city and throughout the nation, activists are rising up against brutal, prejudiced police forces. (p. 1)

In summary, the protest/rally frame informs readers of the efforts that citizens and civil rights leaders are taking to show their condemnation for racial profiling. The frame also highlights organized efforts protestors make to show their feelings on many levels ranging from grassroots to large scale. On one hand, grassroots efforts were as simple as a mother joining Mothers Organized Against Police Terror and voicing her opinions to the media. On the other, large-scale civil rights protests included the Redeem the Dream Rally and the Rev. Al Sharpton's sit-in, which earned him media attention and time in jail. This method of framing is an effective means of attracting supporters and helping people join the cause against racial profiling.

Threat to Civil Liberties

One of the most prominent frames for all publications was racial profiling is a threat to civil liberties, which was common in black press newspapers at 11 and 15 percent before and after September 11, and in mainstream newspapers at 6 and 10 percent before and after September 11. The civil liberties frame discusses the injustice of selectively targeting any group. Articles that included the civil liberties frame generally included sources that acknowledged that Americans have a right to be fearful, but racial profiling is not ever acceptable. Many of the articles included within this frame discussed the injustice of selectively targeting any group. Further, sources in this type of article expressed a deep dislike for racial profiling. For example, a March 6, 2002, Defender article included a statement from a senator who said he was outraged that many blacks and Arab Americans were racially profiled (Strausberg, 2002). The article included this excerpt:

The Rev. Paul Jakes agreed with Conyers that the government is violating Haddad's civil rights, saying his incarceration is a gross violation of due process and civil liberties and an example of the dangerous excess the government continues to commit under the guise of the 'war on terrorism.' (p. 1)

Another example is found in the December 19, 2001, Chicago Defender article that stated a panel of lawyers and civil rights activists denounced the Bush administration's bill to search out terrorists. The group complained that it impinges upon the rights of Americans, will engender racial profiling and will not help to protect people from terrorists. It included the following quote, "We need to stand up for one another. This is not a Muslim issue. It's our issue and don't let the tensions in the Middle East get in the way of all of us protecting one another—Jew and Muslim, white and black" (Strausberg, 2001, p. 18).

In another example, a January 2, 2002, Chicago Defender article applauded civil rights groups for challenging President Bush and U.S. Attorney John Ashcroft and defending the rights of Americans who disagree with the administration's war on Afghanistan or the laws to weed out terrorism that are alleged to engage in racial profiling instead (Strausberg, 2002, p. 3). Other newspapers contained similar examples of the civil liberties threat frame. For example, in response to the measures used to track down and monitor Arabs, a December 17, 2001, Chicago Sun article said the American Civil Liberties Union called the probe "coercive," and some Arab-American groups accused the government of engaging in racial profiling. Further, it stated that police departments refused to cooperate with the FBI (O'Donnell, 2001). The article included this quote:

> We have not committed to helping them conduct those interviews, Chicago police spokesman Dave Bayless said, pointing to a mayoral order that bars police from asking about anyone's immigration status or the nature of their visit to the United States. (p. 18)

A Chicago Sun December 17, 2001, article also discussed the racism that Muslims experienced as they gathered in Chicago to mark the end of Ramadan. It stated that some Muslims were subjected to shouts of "Hey, Osama!" and that school officials joked with them about "terrorists" (O'Donnell, 2001, p. 17). It also included this quote from Jesse Jackson: "Muslim-Americans must not retreat and hide. They must affirm their citizenship; they must affirm their religion. None of us are safe unless all of us are safe" (p. 17).

Similarly, a September 10, 2002, Chicago Defender article stated that not all police and activists are heroes. The article included the following statement: "Many officers, according to Vera Love, the mother of Robert Russ, 'are just as bad as Osama bin Laden. Racial profiling is alive and very prominent in this country, in this city'" (Strausberg, 2002, p.1). Articles also discussed the irony of racial profiling. For example, an April 2, 2002, Chicago Sun-Times editorial said the use of racial profiling is reverse terrorism. The article states: "If we are to root out the evil of terrorism, we must make certain that our efforts don't negate the very principles to which we claim allegiance: justice, truth and freedom" (Dyson, 2002, p. 23).

Repeating History/Slave Era Frame

To provide context and to perhaps color racial profiling in a negative light, many reporters used the repeating history frame to compare September 11 to other events in history. The frame made up 5 percent of the black press articles before the tragedy and 7 percent afterward. For mainstream media, on the other hand, the frame made up 0 percent of articles about racial profiling before September 11 and 2 percent after the event. Examples of the frame included articles that compared racial profiling to the Oklahoma City Bombing and concentration camps. For instance, a September 13, 2001, article in the Chicago Defender warned the United States not to make the mistake it did during the Oklahoma bombing incident during which the media painted suspects as Arabs, but later learned they were white homegrown terrorists (Strausberg, 2001, p. 3). Similarly, a Chicago Defender December 19, 2001, article quotes activist Jesse Jackson as saying, "We did not profile white males after Timothy McVeigh or this young white male who joined the Taliban against the U.S." (p. 18).

In another example, the Chicago Sun-Times on October 2, 2001, explored the idea that the practice is more accepted by Americans now that it focuses on Arab Americans rather than blacks and Hispanics. In the article, a source said:

> We put American citizens of Japanese descent into what amounted to concentration camps. We gave them a day or two notice and they had to uproot themselves from the West Coast. We haven't always lived up to our principles when it comes to treating citizens, who may have some ancestral ties to countries we're presently engaged in hostilities, very well even though they may have been U.S. citizens for generations. (p. 3)

The slave era is the most intriguing historical reference reporters used in their framing of the issue. African-American newspapers made racial profiling more believable and heart wrenching by comparing it to the maladies of slavery. The researcher found an example of this frame in an April 26, 2000, Chicago Defender article, in which a San Francisco State University professor asserted that racial profiling, harsh sentences for black offenders, and police brutality toward people of color still occur because slavery effectively taught whites that black life is cheap (Strausberg, 2000, p. 5). A May 19, 2001, article discussed ongoing efforts to promote awareness and to provide an opportunity for people to present their issues and positions (Strausberg, 2001). It included the following excerpt:

> There is a need to help the public become more aware of our history in terms of slavery, reconstruction, Jim Crowism, racial profiling, police abuse, prosecutorial misconduct, judicial prejudice, redlining, separate but equal, denial of equal opportunity, disproportionate numbers in prison, those on welfare, unemployed, the sick, and why we die sooner than other people. (p. 5)

Another example of this frame was found in the June 27, 2000, Chicago Defender, which stated, "The lingering racial profiling and injustices against blacks in the country are a legacy bequeathed on the country by the Constitution, which was 'racist originally'" (Omoremi, 2000). The article quotes a retired appellate court judge: "The Constitution has 15 provisions, which specifically promote, encourage, legalize and validate slavery" (p. 5).

A January 13, 2000, article stated that a politician believed the mayor's anti-loitering ordinance would further fill up the prisons with mostly blacks (Strausberg, 2000). The politician said, "Today's prisons are like the plantations during slavery. It will do undue stress on my community. This bill is like racial profiling" (p. 6). A December 29, 1999, article included concerns by a senator who called the Safe Neighborhoods Act biased because more African Americans were arrested and charged with felonies while whites were given misdemeanors. The senator also stated that African Americans wanted equal protection under the law (Strausberg, 1999). The article included the following excerpt:

> They took care of the duck hunters, the long guns (rifles) and the bunny rabbits, but they won't take care of Brother Rabbits. They need to understand that we're not animals. We're loving, church-going, God-fearing people. They can't take a few bad people and apply them to the entire Black race. It's these misguided illusions that lead to other problems. They still think we are three-fifths human. (p. 3)

The slave frame continued post-September 11. For example, in one article, the NAACP Chicago South Side Chapter Executive Director Furmin Sessoms said those who tried to end affirmative action for blacks represent the Dred Scott-type of thinking that asserts that blacks have no rights to receive reparations for past and present discriminations. In the Dred Scott decision, the Supreme Court ruled that blacks whose ancestors were deported to this country and were sold as slaves were not members of the political community under the Constitution of the United States. The article included the following excerpt (Strausberg, 2002):

> It is incidents like Judge [Charles Pickering]'s intervention in this case, the federal Appeals Court in NY overturning the (Abner) Louima case, police in Chicago standing up in a court room to intimidate jurors, an epidemic of racial profiling of Blacks, Hispanics, and now Arabs, which are substantial evidence of the badges (of inferiority that are remnants of slavery), and incidents of slavery continues to treat minorities in a way Dred Scott was treated in 1857. . . Dred Scott still lives in the hearts and minds of many who wear black robes and blue suits as well. They deny Blacks equal protection under the law, jobs, and basic human rights. (p. 5)

These examples provide an overview of the slave frame. By comparing racial profiling to the slave era, journalists and sources can successfully convey the message that the practice is wrong.

Necessary Evil Frame/OK in Some Circumstances/Urban Myth

The urban myth frame/necessary evil frame was found in 1 percent of mainstream media articles on racial profiling before and after September 11, and in 0 percent of black press articles before and after the event. Police officers were the primary carriers of this frame. An example is included in a Chicago Sun's June 28, 2000, article that included a quote from a police chief who said, "We thoroughly investigated the incident and found no evidence of official misconduct, the use of excessive force, racial profiling, or denial of medical treatment" (Skertic, 2000, p. 7). Similarly, an August 28, 2001, New York Daily News article discussed assertions by GOP mayoral hopeful Michael Bloomberg who stated that he does not believe racial profiling exists (Saul, 2001). It includes this quote from Bloomberg: "I don't know of any evidence that says there has been [racial profiling] at all. And if that evidence exists, I have never seen it. I just don't believe it. . ." (p. 6).

Some articles in this category described racial profiling as a smart tactic and necessary to prevent future tragedies. For example, George Will, in an April 19 Washington Post column, asserts that the use of race as a criterion in traffic stops is a good idea, as long as it is just "one factor among others in estimating criminal suspiciousness." After the September 11 terrorist attacks on the World Trade Center and the Pentagon, some reporters shifted their focus from the pitfalls of racial profiling to its advantages. For instance, some articles identified racial profiling as a necessary evil in the face of terrorist attacks.

The Human Interest Frame

The human interest frame, which made up 1 percent of black press articles before and after September 11, and 0 and 1 percent of mainstream articles before and after the tragedy, focuses on the plight of racial profiling victims. The human-interest frame is instrumental in putting a face on racial profiling and to counteract the point of view that racial profiling is a justifiable tactic to apprehend deserving criminals.

Upon examining the information, the author identified several trends. For example, reporters often depicted the victims as poor and helpless. Second, such articles frequently used the micro-macro style lead to introduce the larger issue of racial profiling. The Atlanta Journal-Constitution published an article on June 1, 2001, that discussed an airport racial profiling victim whom inspectors stripped, kicked, and force-fed laxatives then checked her bowel movements for drugs. Customs officials found no drugs, and the next day, they released her. The article vividly describes what happened to her as she returned from an international vacation and showed her passport at customs in San Francisco.

Inspectors saw she was born in Colombia and ripped apart her suitcase. Nothing. They took her to a side room and made her strip, kicking her. Finally, they took her to a hospital and force-fed her a laxative, then checked her bowel movements. Customs officials found no drugs. The next day, they released the humiliated woman. Something has to be done about it, said Buritica, 57, of Portchester, N.Y., berating the customs inspectors. Dogs have more intelligence, she said.

In yet another illustration of the human-interest frame, a June 28, 2000, Defender article discussed a victim of racial profiling who was targeted by officers because of his lack of genitalia. Another good example was an August

31, 2003, Defender article that described the details of a 22-year-old Northwestern University football player who police shot to death just 10 days short of his college graduation (Spielman, 2003). The article chronicled the life of his now fatherless son. It included this excerpt:

> Robert Anthony Russ Jr. will turn 4 on Sept. 26 surrounded by the toys, candles, cake and family that are fixtures at most childhood birthday parties. But once again, there'll be somebody missing: the father he will never know. (p. 6)

Poll/Study/Report

Another commonly used frame in newspaper articles was poll/study, which made up 1 and 3 percent of black press articles before and after September 11 and 2 and 11 percent of mainstream media articles before and after the event. The poll frame deals with the findings and statistics from polls and surveys conducted by the media, police departments, and civil liberties organizations. Such articles highlighted various aspects of study findings. For example, The Atlanta Journal and Constitution featured the results of a Gallup Poll on December 11, 1999. The story reported that Americans of all races think profiling is common. In addition, the article said a majority of Americans, regardless of race, believe that racial profiling in police stops is pervasive. In the survey, 77 percent of blacks and 56 percent of whites said they believe the practice is widespread. Polls and surveys are still worthwhile to look at in this analysis. Newspapers must publish such information in order to keep their audiences informed. Furthermore, this frame provides readers with an idea about the pulse of the community and allows them to compare their views with those of their cohorts.

Chapter Six: Discussion

Not surprisingly, previous research has charted differences in how black and mainstream newspapers cover various issues. Such studies have shown variations in article types, frames, and sources. Consequently, this study analyzed how journalists framed the public debate on racial profiling before and after September 11 in those areas. The researcher hypothesized that black press and mainstream media would frame the issue differently because of their respective mission statements, and because of the impact a tragedy such as September 11 would have on the media's framing of any politically charged topic. This was a timely and vital study. The magnitude of the subject matter is illustrated by the fact that some of the catchphrases created and popularized in the media during the event have become permanent fixtures in the English language, i.e. DWB, or "Driving While Black."

Findings indicate, in general, that black and mainstream media differed before and after September 11 in their coverage of racial profiling particularly in their use of sources and ethnic groups. Furthermore, although both newspaper types remained true to their viewpoint, black press was more steadfast in its stance; it continued to focus on racial profiling primarily as a black problem, while mainstream media was more varied in its coverage. One might speculate that sticking to one's charge is especially important for specialized publications such as black press newspapers, which are funded by advertisers who want to reach a specific demographic. Such advertisers may have a problem with the newspaper not speaking to the designated population from their perspective about issues that interest them.

Furthermore, journalists at mainstream newspapers appeared to be swept up in the turmoil and sensationalism of the terrorist attacks. This change in beliefs is illustrated in their coverage of racial profiling as acceptable in the face of a crisis and in articles that questioned whether racial profiling actually exists. Conversely, journalists at black press newspapers printed articles mostly in favor of civil liberties on all accounts—even in the face of a crisis.

Therefore, several factors must be addressed concerning the framing of racial profiling. For example, one must ask why the black press reporters did not waiver in their mission of representing African Americans throughout the coverage of September 11. The researcher speculates that these conclusions are based on four factors—education, religion, politics, and an anti-racist platform. This research provided an opportunity to reach several noteworthy conclusions in the framing of racial profiling. These results will be explored in more detail below.

Ethnic Groups

One example of how September 11 had a greater impact on how mainstream media covered the issue than it had on the black press is how the two groups covered ethnic groups. Prior to September 11, both black and mainstream newspapers tended to focus on African American (and Hispanics to a lesser extent) who had been arrested or pulled over for no reason. This was not a surprise, since prior to September 11 racial profiling was considered a "black" problem, and the issue of racial profiling had been a hot topic in the black community for many years.

Moreover, it made sense for black press newspapers to cover blacks, because historically black press newspapers have spoken to the issues of African Americans. Conversely, Arabs was the least common group covered by both newspapers before September 11. This falls in line with previous research, which shows, in general, newspapers ignore this group. While continuing its coverage of other minorities such as African Americans and Hispanics, after September 11 mainstream media focused primarily on Arabs.

This stance falls in line with its mission, which is to attract readers from the general population. The huge increase in coverage of Arabs after the event can be explained by the September 11 tragedy coupled with the racially charged environment that motivated the media to broaden the term "racial profiling" to include Arabs, Middle Easterners, and Muslims. Such articles centered on specific incidents in which victims from these groups were harassed physically and mentally by various law enforcers as well as American citizens. On the other hand, black press newspapers continued to focus predominantly on African Americans after September 11; however, a small percentage of its articles focused on Arabs. One explanation for this small shift is the black press did not have a choice but to present the news of the day. To ignore September

11 and the impact it had on Arabs, Muslims, and many other ethnic groups would have been unimaginable. The black press was forced to include other ethnic groups in its coverage in order to stay current.

The media, in general, increased the visibility of Middle Easterners after the terrorist attacks, creating an environment in which both African Americans and mainstream reporters possibly felt their security was in jeopardy. However, reporters did a pretty good job of differentiating between Arabs, Muslims, and persons from Arab-speaking countries. Before conducting the study, the researcher thought this would present a problem as citizens often lump members of these groups into one category, especially when referring to terrorist-related issues. Most of the articles in the sample focused on Arab Americans. However, if the article referred to religion, the reporters usually specified that the person's religion. Similarly, if the article dealt with persons of other races or ethnic groups, the press specifically pointed this out. For example, if an Asian was asked to leave a flight because a pilot perceived him as a threat, articles identified this person as such.

The researcher speculates that perhaps this finding is due to guidelines set forth by the Society of Professional Journalists (SPJ) after September 11 to help to ward off racial profiling in news coverage. On October 6, 2001, at its National Convention in Seattle, the Society of Professional Journalists passed a resolution that urged journalists to portray Muslims, Arabs, Middle Eastern and South Asian Americans in the richness of their diverse experiences. It also encouraged reporters to seek out and include Arabs and Arab Americans, Muslims, South Asians, and men and women of Middle Eastern descent in all stories about the war, not just those about Arab and Muslim communities or racial profiling (SPJ, 2002).

Sources

Frames by sources structure the understanding of social phenomena by defining the roles varied individuals, groups, organizations, and institutions play. In general, the study found that before September 11, popular sources for black press newspapers were civil rights activists, attorneys, and law enforcers. In line with previous research, such sources were probably deemed reliable or "elite" in the black community. Conversely, mainstream press tended to frame activists and legislators as the movers and shakers. In line with previous findings from this study that demonstrate that the black press did not waiver post-September 11. After the event, the most popular category for black press was still civil rights agency representative, while the most popular source for mainstream media switched to citizen. Consistency for the black press is easy to explain; it remained true to its platform, which is to speak to black issues from a black perspective. But the findings for the mainstream media are not so cut and dry. Perhaps citizens became more important in the face of a crisis because the mainstream media wanted to show that this heated issue touched many lives. The use of elite sources such as politicians and city officials would not demonstrate this perspective.

These findings fall in line with the Domke, et al. (2003) research mentioned earlier, which found that for the five months before and after September 11, most Arab American and African American sources spoke as individuals rather than government officials or non-government opinion leaders. Further parallelisms between the two studies cannot be drawn because the present researcher of the present study chose to look at the race of people mentioned in articles rather than the race of sources interviewed. This choice was made because the race of sources is difficult to assess unless it is explicitly outlined in the article. Most articles did not specifically say the source's race, i.e., John Smith, an African American. Rather they discussed the issue and the story was about a specific racial profiling incident such as John Smith being pulled over because he was African American, then they mentioned his or her race.

Sources were interesting to study because findings illustrate a frame contest in which two parties representing opposing viewpoints hash it out in the press (Gamson, Crouteau, Hoynes & Sasson, 1992). Opponents were: police officers, who wanted readers to believe racial profiling does not exist; and civil rights agencies and leaders, who wanted to get the word out about the injustices done by police officers. By having their quotes featured in newspaper articles members of both groups were able to move forward their messages and beliefs. For example, from the latter group, the Civil Liberties Union was the most visible organization quoted in articles. In fact, many articles discussed the June 1999 report, in which the ACLU documented the widespread phenomenon of "Driving While Black or Brown." In addition, several articles detailed lawsuits filed by the American Civil Liberties Union (ACLU) on behalf of minorities. Reporters also turned to the National Association for the Advancement of Colored People and the Southern Christian Leadership Conference organization for information about the topic. Such organizations were responsible for starting grassroots organizations to help end racial profiling in their communities. Notable civil rights spokespersons that had the same agenda included the Rev. Jesse Jackson and Martin Luther King III, the son of the late Dr. Martin Luther King, and New York activist Rev. Al Sharpton.

In addition, the framing package of choice for both groups was "legislation." The commonality of this frame may be explained in part by the need to end racial profiling and also in response to the agenda set by civil rights activists such as the Rev. Jesse Jackson and Al Sharpton. The two initiated efforts such as rallies and editorials to expose the practice and perhaps lead to its abolishment. This finding is important because Gamson and Lasch (1983) contend that the ideas that appear in news are best understood as media packages that feature a central organizing idea for events and use framing devices that support the main idea of the story.

This study's conclusions raise the important question of whether reporters give voice to viewpoints that reflect the prevailing newsroom standard. The answer is probably yes because before September 11, the most common source for black press was civil rights agency representative, which makes sense if the black press' mission statement is to focus on issues relevant to African-Americans. During the early years of the drug war, which led to more instances of racial profiling, it was of utmost importance before September 11 to let

African Americans know that such a problem existed, as well as the tactics available to protect their civil rights. Civil rights agency representatives were able to this. The fact that the most popular source for black press remained civil right's representatives after September 11 illustrates that the black press' agenda did not change after the horrendous event. Its primary goal was to still inform and educate African Americans about the pertinent issues of the day from a black perspective. Mainstream reporters, on the other hand, perhaps wanted to present the issue from the man-on-the-street perspective, or in the vein that this happens predominantly to minorities and average people, so who best to interview but citizens.

This look at sources is important because reporters may use them to effectively create the illusion of validity or factuality. Reporters can add credibility to certain points of view by quoting official sources, and marginalize certain points of view by relating a quote or point of view to a social deviant. Furthermore, under one frame, based on quotes or sources, a particular group may be seen as an essential actor in resolving a social problem, while in another the same group may be perceived as unimportant (Hertog & McLeod, 1999).

Education, Demographics, and Audience Served

Newspaper audiences obviously impact how newspapers frame certain issues. The fact that African-American and mainstream newspapers are aimed at different populations helps explain why they contain different frames. On the most obvious level, if newspapers don't serve their demographics, they will lose their readers not to mention their advisers as mentioned about. Demographics become important when a newspaper decides what side it's going to take in its coverage of an issue. The black press chose to continue its coverage of racial profiling as a social injustice aimed primarily at African Americans because this is what their readers and advertisers paid to read and see in their newspapers. If they wanted a different point of view, they would have picked up a mainstream newspaper.

In addition, readers and journalists at black newspapers, on the whole, are far more educated than the general population. This may be assumed based on the self descriptions of some of the black newspapers used in this sample, which said their readers are well-educated and financially stable. The average person does not read black media because it is harder to find than mainstream media; there is not a newsstand containing them on every corner, and they are not sold at chain supermarkets. Furthermore, the circulation rates for black newspapers are low, and there are only a few black dailies left in the country. People who make an effort to seek out black media are usually focused and dedicated to the black cause. Such readers are usually dedicated because they are searching for in-depth reporting that focuses on fairness in reporting from a black perspective. These facts help explain why black press newspapers did not waiver in their coverage of the issue when the order of the day was to be afraid of Arabs. Members of this particular demographic would not change sides on such an issue as racial profiling because to do so would go against the very foundation of black newspapers—civil rights.

This fact helps answer another key fact that must be addressed: the polls indicated that African Americans favored racial profiling after the September 11 terrorist attacks. For example, a Boston Globe poll found African-Americans are more likely than other racial groups to favor profiling and stringent airport security checks for Arabs and Arab Americans (Scales, 2001). Yet, this view did not manifest itself in black publications. Perhaps the education level of citizens poll takers interviewed versus those who actually read or write for black press newspapers is significantly different. The average person interviewed for a poll, may be less educated than black press readers and writers; and the less educated citizen may be unfamiliar with walking a party line or remain loyal to one's beliefs. In addition, poll findings may have been swayed by the responses of African Americans who were glad that another group was finally under scrutiny by the mainstream media. One of the most common responses of African Americans who hear news about a shooting or any type of violence on television is usually trepidation and the fear that the person is probably black. As a result, some African Americans felt relieved that another group was under the microscope temporarily. This was illustrated in one of the articles mentioned in this studies literature review, in which the writer said finally another group is under the microscope. We can take our eyes off O.J. Simpson and Mike Tyson and now focus on Mohammad, etc.

In addition, the author speculates that this discrepancy may be explained by the black press' sense of responsibility to their audience. Even though some journalists may believe racial profiling is an adequate tool for apprehending terrorists, they may be reluctant to portray Middle Easterners unfairly. Additionally, the black press may believe that to go against the basic tenet on which they were founded is both unprofessional and hypocritical. Such journalists may perceive that it is unethical to advocate racial profiling of any group.

For whatever reason, the black press did a good job of sticking to its platform even during a time of crisis and when personal safety became an issue for every American. Two frames were used by the groups to illustrate this point—the repeating history/slave frame for the black press and the necessary evil frame for the mainstream media. These conclusions are noteworthy because these two frames are almost polar extremes. For example, the slave frame presented in black newspapers was produced possibly in response to the urban myth frame in mainstream newspapers.

African-American newspapers made racial profiling believable and sad by comparing it to the maladies of slavery. For readers of black publications, its comparison to racial profiling provides cultural resonance, which refers to the degree that journalists package news in accordance with the beliefs, stories, and imagery that coincide with the dominant culture of their society. On the other hand, this particular frame might not be as effective for mainstream media, because its fragmented audience might not relate to the stress and strife that coincided with that particular period in history.

Likewise, the mainstream media have two reasons for yielding to the urban myth frame. First, mainstream reporters and editors may actually believe that blacks are more likely to commit crimes; and secondly, they must print what they think their audience and advertisers prefer to read. Mainstream reporters and editors are more likely to believe the negative stereotypes that they write in newspapers and observe on television about minorities and feel that racial profiling is an acceptable way to cut back on crime and keep their neighborhoods safe. Therefore, for mainstream media this frame supports the status quo.

Religion, Politics, and Society

The two types of newspapers might also take this stand based on religious beliefs. African Americans as a whole tend to rely on clergy for guidance and representation during tragedies such as the terrorist attacks. During September 11, many people from a religious background viewed racial profiling as a religious issue rather than a safety issue. Profiling people goes against the basic tenet of Christianity, which is to love thy neighbor. In a nutshell, the two ideas contradict themselves. Such an opposing stand would have been fleshed out and discussed in newsrooms before black reporters and editors printed stories running counter to their mission statement. Furthermore, the large population of black Muslims in the United States helped African Americans see the issue from another group's perspective even in the face of a major crisis.

Politics is another explanation for the differences in black and mainstream media. As mentioned in the literature review, black press often takes the view of the Democratic Party, while mainstream media often takes on the view of the Republican Party. Although this assertion may not be necessarily true for mainstream media, it is undeniable, that the black press generally identifies with Democratic viewpoints rather than with views from any other political party. Such views include inclusiveness, economic development, and personal freedoms for persons of all races and genders. Therefore, the view that racial profiling may be OK in some circumstances may have been perceived as a Republican Party stance. In response to such a view, it would be prudent for the black press to respond by saying such a tactic is wrong.

Similarly, political correctness was at its height in popularity during this period; therefore, it would be social suicide for any publication to advocate taking away the basic rights of American citizens. Another reason for this conclusion is the fall out from several high-profile cases, such as the beating of Rodney King.

Future Studies

The study has important implications for mass media scholars who have long argued that it is important to understand the ways in which the journalistic framing of issues occurs. Such framing influences public understanding and, consequently, policy formation. Furthermore, many of these findings were not surprising because history has shown that gatekeepers at mainstream and black press outlets have different ideas or perceptions of what is important and what should be covered in their respective news outlets.

framing of issues occurs. Such framing influences public understanding and, consequently, policy formation. Furthermore, many of these findings were not surprising because history has shown that gatekeepers at mainstream and black press outlets have different ideas or perceptions of what is important and what should be covered in their respective news outlets.

The findings from this research set the stage for future studies. For example, it would be of importance to analyze other topics of interest such as affirmative action, hate crimes and gay marriage using the same frames established in this study. It would be interesting to discern whether other stories contain similar frames. Of particular interest to the researcher is if the slave frame has been used in conjunction with other issues. In other studies, one may seek to find out if shorter intervals alter the outcome of frames used for racial profiling. The author speculates that the time span of three years may possibly have been too long to judge whether September 11 made a difference in the media's coverage of racial profiling. With a shorter time span, the two newspapers may have proven more alike in their framing of the issue. However, three years gave each publication enough time to forget about the tragedy and to begin pursuing the different frames. This method may help assess if the two media types were more similar immediately following September 11, reverting back to their original stance once the tragedy calmed down.

A different approach will be needed if researchers are to identify newsroom norms and the factors that determine which topics will attract the attention of journalists and win the support of their editors. The researcher recommends that follow-up studies include feedback from editors and reporters as the study of this issue would be greatly aided with qualitative in-depth interviews with the reporters and editors of these media. Hence, a survey component could be added to the study to find out if they consciously decided to frame the issue a certain way. Such a study could also address other issues such as how newsroom, values, etc. translate into different frames.

Future studies on this topic might also explore how other regional newspapers covered the issue and look at the dynamics at work based on the newspaper's location. For example, Detroit would be a good location for a separate study on the topic because of its large population of Arabs.

Another interesting angle might be to compare elite with non-elite newspapers. This would allow for a better understanding of how news is read within a specific social context. It would also allow the researcher to take the next step and see if the news coverage as written brings a reader to a specific action.

Conclusions

While both newspaper types remained true to their missions, black press was more steadfast in its aim to provide the black perspective for its readers. It focused on racial profiling primarily as a black problem, while mainstream media was more diverse in its coverage. After September 11, it switched its focus primarily to Arabs and cases that dealt with 9/11. Also worth reiterating is the fact that many of the frames the newspapers used to cover the issue of racial profiling were actually in opposition. For example, the slave frame presented in black newspapers was produced possibly in response to the urban myth frame in mainstream newspapers. African-American newspapers made racial profiling more believable and heart-wrenching by comparing it to the maladies of slavery. On the contrary, mainstream media made the myth frame more believable by quoting sources who pointed out that we had no statistics to show that racial profiling actually happens.

The conclusions from this study demonstrate the idea that the black press is based on the ever-present notion that the constructs of American society are racist or its articles are written from a white person's perspective. Although the mainstream press may not be racist, they often are written primarily for a white audience. Therefore, one of the primary goals of the black press is to counteract many of the ideas that are presented in the mainstream media. Black press reporters and editors have the everyday reality of living in a racist society that often presents African Americans in a negative light. As a result, it is the black press' job to present the flip-side of this coverage and to report news from a different perspective that favors African American people.

Based on this idea, whether true or not, the black press had no choice but to take the stance that racial profiling is wrong. During the politically charged period following September 11, black press journalists embraced a fair and balanced doctrine and were reluctant to go on record in support of stories that may be misconstrued as racist in nature, i.e. in support of the racial profiling of any group. To advocate the racial profiling of any other group, whether it be Arab or Hispanic would not be a smart business or journalistic move. Perhaps editors and reporters at black newspapers knew that even if their readers agreed that Arabs should be racial profiled in the face of a crisis, it would not be prudent to print such commentary in a publication that is based on promoting civil rights and a democratic society. As a result, the black press chose to publish the day's news fairly and accurately from the African-American point of view.

These conclusions are significant because frames structure understanding of social phenomena by defining the roles varied individuals, groups, organizations, and institutions play. Under one frame, a particular group may be seen as an essential actor in resolving a social problem, while in another the same group may be perceived as unimportant.

Furthermore, this study has implications for the argument of whether black newspapers are necessary in today's society. The researcher concludes with a resounding, "yes." Although newspapers strive to be objective in their selections of sources, frames, and emphasis, it is impossible as detailed earlier in this study. People come to newsrooms with their own set of values, preconceived notions, and ethics. Additionally, journalists at each newspaper type learn the written and unwritten rules from the feedback they receive from editors and customers. Until the gap that divides African Americans and other readers lessens, black press newspapers will remain an important staple in the black community. And unless this happens, there will always be a need for black publications to ensure that all sides of issues such as racial profiling are covered fairly and from the black perspective.

Bibliography

Ali, M. (2003). Arab/Muslim 'Otherness': The role of racial constructions in the gulf war and the continuing crisis with Iraq. Journal of Muslim Minority Affairs, 22 (1), 131.

Bagdikian, B. H. (1969). The press and its crisis of identity. Mass media in a free society. Lawrence: University of Kansas Press.

Barsamian, D. (2000). Eqbal Ahmad – "Confronting Empire" Interviews with by David Barsamian: South End Press.

Belau, J.M. (1978). Images of Arabs and Israelis in the Prestige Press: 1966 - 1974. Journalism Quarterly, 55, 732-733 & 799.

Bellinger, L. (2002). A New Farrakhan? The Nation of Islam leans toward the mainstream. Sojourners. May/June 2002

Berkowitz, L., and K. H. Rogers (1986). A priming effect analysis of media influences. In J. Bryant & D. Zillman (eds.), Perspectives on media effects. Hillsdale, NJ: Erlbaum: 57-81.

Baylor, T. (1996). Media framing of movement protest: The case of American Indian protest. Social Science Journal, 33(3), 241.

Berry & Manning-Miller, C. (1996). Mediated messages and African-American culture: contemporary Issues. Thousand Oaks, CA: Sage.

Brennen, B (2002). CCS ideological critique of the other. AEJMC Paper Presentation.

Brunt, C. (Oct. 17, 2001). Bigots turn from blacks to Arab-Americans. The Omaha World-Herald Company.

Callahan, G. and Anderson, W. (2001). Roots of Racial Profiling. Reason Magazine. reason.com/0108/fe.gc.the.shtml

Campbell, E. (1995). Race, Myth and the News. Thousand Oaks, Calif.: Sage Publications

Carragee, K.M. (1997). Framing, the news media, and collective action. Paper presented at The Conference for the Center for Mass Communication Research "Framing the New Media Landscape." Columbia, S.C., October 13-14, 1997.

Christison, K. (1987). The Arab in Recent Popular Fiction. Middle East Journal (Summer 1987).

Chomsky, N. & Herman, S. (1988). Manufacturing Consent: The Political Economy of the Mass Media. New York: Pantheon Books.

Chon, M. and Arzt, D. (2005). Walking while Muslim. Law & Contemp. Probs., 68, 215

Citizen Complaint Review Board. (2002). Racial Profiling In Washington, DC. http://www. occr.dc.gov January 7, 2002

Coke, T. (2003). Racial profiling after9/11: Old story, new debate, in lost liberties, (ed.) Cynthia Brown. New York: The New Press, p. 9

Colangelo, L. (September 7, 2001). Rudy signs bill to release info on stop-frisks_ New York Daily News, p. 25

Crouch, S. (June 18, 2003). It's Not Profiling, It's Good Policing. The Washington Post.

D'Angelo, P. (2002). News framing as a multi-paradigmatic research program: A response to Entman. Journal of Communication, 52(4), 870-888.

Dates, J. L. & Barlow, W. (1993). Split Image: African-Americans in the Mass Media (second edition). Howard University Press, Washington, D.C.

Dates, J. L. & Pease, E. C. (1994). Warping the World: Media's Mangled Images Of Race. The Freedom Forum Media Studies. Columbia University, New York, 8 (3) 81-88.

De la Cruz, G. P. and Brittingham, A. (2003). The Arab Population: 2000 Census 2000 Brief

Derbyshire, J. (2001). In Defense of Racial Profiling. National Review 53 (3), 38-40.

Dickerson, D. (2003). Framing political Correctness. Reese, S., Gandy, O. and Grant, (Eds.). Framing Public Life: Perspectives on Media and our Understanding of the Social World. (Mahwah, N.J.: Lawrence Erlbaum, 2001).

Dimmick, J. (1974). The gatekeeper: an uncertainty theory. Journalism Monographs, November.

Domke, et al. (2003). "Insights into U.S. racial hierarchy: Racial profiling, news sources, and September 11." Journal of Communication 53(4): 606-623.

Dridi, D. (November 19, 2002). *Converts say Islam has given their lives structure.* The Seattle AfterIntelligencer.

Druckman, J. N. (2001). On the limits of framing effects: Who can frame? Journal of Politics, 63(4), 1041.

Dyson, M. (April 2, 2002). *No justice in reverse.* Chicago Sun Times, p. 23

Dyson, M. (February 26, 2002). *Sharpton's on point.* Chicago Sun Times, p. 23

Edelman, M. (1993). Contestable categories and public opinion. Political Communication, 10, 231-242.

Eisenberg, C. (January 24, 2005). Black Muslims seek acceptance from fellow Americans, adherents. Newsday, New York City

Elder, L. (April 22, 2001). Rushing to judgment over racial profiling. FrontPageMagazine.com

Entman, R.M. (1989). How the media affect what people think: an information processing approach. The Journal of Politics, 51(2), 347.

Entman, R. (1990). Modern racism and the images of Blacks in local television. Critical Studies in Mass Communication 7:332-345.

Entman, R.M. (1992). African-Americans in the news: Television, modern racism and cultural change. Journalism Quarterly, 69(2), 341-361.

Entman, R.M. (1991). Framing U.S. coverage of international news: contrasts in narratives of the KAL and Iran air incidents. Journal of Communication, 41 (4), 6-27.

Entman, R.M. (1993). Framing: toward clarification of a fractured paradigm. Journal of Communication, 43 (4), 51-58.

Entman, R.M. and Rojecki, A. (2000). The black image in the white mind: media and race in America. University of Chicago Press.

Fedler, F. (1973). The media and minority groups. A study of access. Journalism Quarterly. 50, 109-17.

Fellows, J. (Jan/Feb, 1998). Meet the black press. Washington Monthly, Vol. 30 Issue ½, p10.

Foner, E. (1998). Reconstruction: America's unfinished revolution. New York: Harper & Row, 199–201.

Foucault, M. (1980). Power/knowledge: selected interviews and other writings 1972-1977, (ed) Colin Gordon, Harvester, London.

Gallup Organization (2001). Terrorism Most Important, But Americans Remain Upbeat.

Gamson, W.A. (1985). Goffman's legacy to political sociology. Theory & Society 14, p. 605–22

Gamson, W. A. and Modigliani, A. (1987). The changing culture of affirmative action. In Braungart, R.G. and Braungart, M.M. (eds.), Research in Political Sociology, 3, London, England, 137-177.

Gamson, W.A., Crouteau, D., Hoynes, W., & Sasson, T. (1992). Media images and the social construction of reality. Annual Review of Sociology, 18(1), 373.

Gamson, W.A. & Lasch, K. (1983). The Political Culture of Social Welfare Policy. In Evaluating the Welfare State: Social and Political Perspectives, ed. Shimon E.

Shapiro and Ephraim Yuchtman-Yaar. New York: New York Academic Press. p. 397-415.

Gandy, O. (1996). If it weren't for bad luck: Framing stories of racially comparative risk, in V. Berry & C. Manning-Miller (Eds.). Mediated messages and African-American culture: Contemporary issues. Thousand Oaks, CA: Sage, p. 55-75

Gandy, O. (1998). Communication and race: A structural perspective. New York, Oxford

Gandy, O. (2002). Framing comparative risk. Paper for Presentation at the Psychology and Social Psychology Section IAMCR Conference, Barcelona.

Gandy, O. H. & Baruh, L. (2005). Racial Profiling: They Said It Was Against the Law! University of Ottawa Law & Technology Journal.

Gans, H. J. (1979). Deciding What's News. New York: Vintage Books.

Gieber, W. (1954). Across the desk: a study of 16 telegraph editors. Journalism Quarterly. 1954, 61-68.

Gieber, W. (1960). How the "gatekeepers" view local civil liberties news. Journalism Quarterly. 37, 199-205.

Gilliam, F D. Jr., S. Iyengar, Simon, A. and Wright, O. (1996). Crime in black and white: the violent, scary world of local news. Harvard International Journal of Press/Politics. 1: 6-23.

Gitlin, Todd. (1980). The Whole World is Watching Berkeley, University of California Press.

Graber, D. (1988). Processing the News: How People Tame the Information Tide, 2nd ed., Longman, New York.

Gramsci, A. (1971). Selections from the Prison Notebooks. Edited by Q. Hoare and G. N. Smith. New York: International Publishers.

Gunther, A.C. (1998). The persuasive press inference [Electronic version]. Communication Research, 25, 486-505.

Hackett, G. (1985). Role of mathematics self-efficacy in the choice of math-related majors of college women and men. A path analysis. Journal of Counseling Psychology. 32, 47-56.

Hall, S. (1980). Cultural Studies: Two Paradigms. Media, Culture, and Society, 2 57-72.

Harris, D. (1999). Driving While Black: Racial Profiling on our Nation's Highways. New York: ACLU, 1999.

Hartmann, P., & Husband, C. (1974). Racism and the mass media: A study of the role of the mass media in the formation of white beliefs and attitudes in Britain. Totowa, NJ: Rowman & Littlefield.

Harvard Civil Rights-Civil Liberties Law Review. (2004). 39, 1, Thirteenth Amendment Framework for Combating Racial Profiling

Hertog, J.K., and McLeod, D. M. (1999). Social control, social change and the mass media's role in the regulation of protest groups. In David Demers and K. Viswanath (Eds.) Mass Media, Social Control, and Social Change: A Macrosocial Perspective. Ames, IA: Iowa State University. Iowa State Univ. Press.

Irwin, W. (1970). Propaganda and the news or what makes you think so? Westport, CT: Greenwood.

Iyengar, S. and D. R. Kinder (1987). News That Matters. Chicago: Univ. of Chicago Press, p. 33.

Janowitz, M. (1985). Professional models in journalism: The gatekeeper and the advocate. Journalism Quarterly, 52(4).

Jhally, S., & Lewis, J. (1992). Enlightened Racism: The Cosby Show, Audiences and the Myth of the American Dream. Boulder: Westview Press.

Johnson, P. (1992, December). The media and truth: Is there a moral duty [Electronic version] Current, 4-8.

Katz, E., & Lazarsfeld, P. F. (1960). Personal Influence. New York: The Free Press.

Kasravi, N. (2004). Threat and Humiliation. Racial Profiling, Domestic Security, and Human Rights in the United States. Amnesty International USA Publications.

Keeter, S. and Burke Olsen, "Views of Islam Remain Sharply Divided." The Pew Research Center for the People and the Press, September 9, 2004, http://people-press.org/commentary/pdf/96.pdf.

Keeter, S. (2005). Fewer say Islam encourages violence views of Muslim-Americans old steady after London bombings, http://www.pewtrusts.com/pdf/PRC_muslims_0705.pdf

Kennedy, R. (1999). Suspect Policy, The New Republic 30, 33 (September 13 & 20, 1999).

Kinsley, M. (September 28, 2001). Racial profiling at the airport: discrimination we're afraid to be against. Slate Magazine.

Krauthammer, C. (2001). The Case for Profiling. Time, March. 18.

Lamb, C. (1999). L'affaire Jake Powell: the minority press goes to bat against segregated baseball. Journalism & Mass Communication Quarterly, 76 (1), p21.

Legislative   Reports.   Daily   Report   Number   31   March   12,   2004 legis.state.ga.us/legis/2003_04/house/.../daily wraps/daily 31.htm

Lewin, K. (1947). Frontiers in group dynamics: 11 channels of group life: social planning and action research. Human Relations, 1, 145-146.

Li, X. & Izard, R. (2003). Media in a Crisis Situation Involving National Interest: A Content Analysis of Major U.S. Newspapers' and TV Networks' Coverage of the 9/11 Tragedy. Newspaper Research Journal, Vol. 24, No.1, Winter 2003

Lombardi, F. (August 21, 2001). *Racial profiling foes fear it isn' t enough.* New York Daily News.

Lule, J. (1995). The rape of Mike Tyson: Race, the press and symbolic types. Critical Studies in Mass Communication, 12, 176-195.

Mark, S. & Brooks, S. & Mehta, S. (2003). *Have We Learned the Lessons of History? Immigration* Policy Focus, vol. 1, 3.

Malkin, M. (August 17, 2004). *Racial profiling: A matter of survival.* USA Today,

Martin, R. (August 16, 2005). *We must support Black media now more than ever.* Chicago Defender.

Martindale, C. (1986). The White Press and Black America. New York: Greenwood Press.

Martindale, C. (1990). Changes in newspaper images of African-Americans. Newspaper Research Journal 11(1), 46-48.

Maxwell, K. A., J. Huxford, et al. (2000). "Covering Domestic Violence: How the O.J Simpson. Case Shaped Reporting of Domestic Violence in the News Media." Journalism and Mass Communication Quarterly 77(2): 258-272.

McCoy, L. (May 9, 2000). *Mothers to march against police brutality.* Philadelphia Tribune. p. 6C

McKinnon, J. (2000). The Black Population: 2000 Census 2000 Brief U.S. Department of Commerce Economics and Statistics Administration U.S. CENSUS BUREAU

Meeks, K. (2000). Driving While Black: What To Do If You Are a Victim of Racial Profiling. Random House, Inc.

Melton, R.H. (Jan. 11, 2001). *Warner Seeks to Ban Racial Profiling; Virginia Governor-Elect Promises Initiatives That Fit Within Tighter Budget.* Washington Post.

Merskin, D. (2004). The Construction of Arabs as Enemies: After September 11 Discourse of George W. Bush. Mass Communication & Society, 7(2), p157.

Messner, M. & Solomon, S. (1993). Outside the Frame: Newspaper Coverage of the Sugar Ray Leonard Wife Abuse Story. Sociology of Sport Journal 10: 119-134.

Mitchell, M. (October 2, 2001).

Moss, J. (2001). Americans Fear Hostility After Algerian Arrests. ABCNEW.COM.

Mott, F. L. (1941). American Journalism, Macmillan. The most detailed general reference book on the topic, a one-volume library.

Nelson, T. E., Zoe M. Oxley, and Rosalee A. Clawson. (1997). Toward A New Press, 2002.

Neuman, W. R., Just, M. R., & Crigler, A. N. (1992). Common knowledge. Chicago: University of Chicago Press.

O'Donnell, M. (December 17, 2001). *Muslims tell of taunting, harassment after September 11*. Chicago Sun-Times, p. 17.

Omoremi, J. (June 27, 2000). *Pincham American Constitution racist*. Chicago Defender. Chicago, Ill.: p. 5

Pan, Z, & Kosicki, G. (1993). Framing analysis: An approach to news discourse. Political Communication, 10, 55-75.

Parenti, M. (1997). Methods of media manipulation. Humanist, 57(4), 5.

Parker, E. (1997). PR Goes to War: The Effects of Public Relations Campaigns on Media Framing of the Kuwaiti and Bosnian Crises. AEJMC Conference Papers.

Polakow-Suransky, S. (2001). Flying While Brown. The American Prospect, Inc. National Review, Oct 14, 2002.

Project for Excellence in Journalism. (2004). Overview. The State of the News Media 2004: An Annual Report on American Journalism. Retrieved on April 13, 2004 from: http://www.stateofthenewsmedia.org/2004/

Project for Excellence in Journalism. (n.d.). A Statement of Shared Purpose. Retrieved on April 13, 2004, from: http://www.journalism.org/resources/ guidelines/principles/purpose.asp

Pulcini, T. (1993). Trends in research on Arab Americans. Journal of American Ethnic History 12, 4.

Ragin, C.C. (1992). Introduction: Cases of What is a Case? In C.C. Ragin & H.S. Becker (Eds), What is a Case? Exploring the Foundation of Social Inquiry, p. 1-17. New York: Cambridge University Press.

Ramasastry (2002). Airplane security: Terrorism prevention or racial profiling?

Ramirez, D., McDevitt, J., Farrell, A. (2000). A resource guide on racial profiling data collection systems. Retrieved from the World Wide Web: www.doj.org

Ratzlaff, A. & Iorio, S. (1994). Paper presented at the Qualitative Studies Division at the annual meeting of the Association for Education in Journalism and Mass Communication, Washington, D.C., Aug. 7-9, 1994.

Reese, S.D. (1997). Framing public life: A bridging model for media study. Paper presented at The Conference for the Center for Mass Communication.

Riffe, D., Ellis, B., Rogers, M. K., Van Ommeren, R. L. and Woodman, K. A. (1986). Gatekeeping and the Network News Mix. Journalism Quarterly 63, 315–21.

Rowley, K. (2003). Separate and still unequal: A comparative study of blacks in business magazines. Journal of Communications, 14(4), p245.

Ruffins, P. (August 06, 2000). Why cops need policing on brutality, profiling; Two authors recount acts of racial injustice, p. 12.

Ruklick, J. (Feb. 21, 2000). *Court weighs racial profiling*. Chicago Defender; p. 1.

Ruklick, J. (June 6, 2000). *Call to redeem the dream*. Chicago Defender, p. 1

Said, E (2001) Time for a change of policy. Al-Ahram Weekly Online 15(21), 560.

Saul, M. (August 28, 2001). *No racial profiling here, mike says; Ferrer scoffs*. New York Daily News, p. 17

Saito, N. (2002). Whose Liberty? Whose Security? Oregon Law Review, at (Westlaw 81 Or. L. Rev. 1051).

Scales, A. (September 3, 2001). Polls say *African-Americans tend to favor checks.* Boston Globe.

Schramm, W. (1955). How Communication Works. The Process Effects of Mass Communication. U. Of Illinois. 3-26.

Semetko, H. A., & Valkenburg, P. M. (2000). Framing European politics: A content analysis of press and television news. Journal of Communication. 50, 93-109.

Shaheen, J. G. (1984). The TV Arab. Bowling Green, OH: Bowling Green State University Press.

Shoemaker, P. (1984). Media treatment of deviant political groups. Journalism Quarterly, 61; 66-75.

Shoemaker, P. J. (1991) Communication Concepts 3: gatekeeping Newbury Park, CA: Sage Publications.

Shoemaker, Pamela J. and Reese, Stephen D. (1996) Mediating the Message: theories of influences on mass media content, 2nd edn, White Plains, NY: Longman

Sigel, L. V. (1973). Reporters and officials: the organization of newsmaking. Lexington: D.C. Heath & Co.

Snider, Paul B. Mr. Gates revisited. Journalism Quarterly. 1967, 419-427

Southwell, D. (January 11, 2000). *Divided residents applaud vote to hire investigator.* Chicago Sun-Times, p 7.

SPJ (2001). Guidelines for Countering Racial, Ethnic and Religious Profiling: https://www.spj.org/divguidelines.asp? <accessed Sept. 9, 2006>.

Squires, C. and Brouwer, D. (2002). In/Discernible bodies: the politics of passing in dominant and marginal media. Critical Studies in Media Communication (19) 3, 283–310.

St. Clair, D. Tajima, A. (2003). The Road to War: Breaking the Code Presented at the Critical and Cultural Studies Division, AEJMC - April 1, 2003.

Stanley, D.L. (Jun 9, 2001). *Racial Profiling Legislation Reintroduced.* Atlanta Inquirer, p. 1

Steward, D. & Totman, M. (2005). Don't Mind if I Take a Look, Do Ya? An Examination of Consent Searches and Hit Rates at Texas Traffic Stops.

Strausberg, C (June 14, 2001). *Lawyer wins 1st federal TRO in racial profiling case* Chicago Defender, p. 7.

Strausberg, C. (Dec 29, 1999). *Hendon vows to vote against 'bias' crime bill.* Chicago Defender, p. 3.

Strausberg, C. (Jan 13, 2000). *Beavers probes high drop in Black cop candidates.* Chicago Defender. p. 6.

Strausberg, C. (Apr 11, 2000). *Durbin report says Black women targeted by Customs* Chicago Defender, p. 4

Strausberg, C. (Apr 26, 2000). *Police brutality vs. Blacks blamed on vestiges of slavery* Chicago Defender. p. 5

Strausberg, C. (Dec 19, 2001). *Anti-terrorist bill dunked at debate* Chicago Defender, p. 18.

Strausberg, C. (January 13, 2000). *Highland Park cops seek protection in racial conflict* Chicago Defender, p. 1.

Strausberg, C. (Mar 7, 2002). *NAACP Likens Pickering to Dred Scott.* Chicago Defender, p. 5.

Strausberg, C. (May 19, 2001). *Davis holds Reparations town hall meeting Saturday* Chicago Defender, p. 5.

Strausberg, C. (Oct 2, 2001). *Atty. Willis: 'Osama bin Laden should not surrender'* Chicago Defender, p. 3

Strausberg, C. (Sep 13, 2001). *Jesse, interfaith group warn U.S. against Racial Profiling* Chicago Defender, p. 3

Strausberg, C. (Dec 19, 2001) *Anti-terrorist bill dunked at debate.* Chicago Defender, p. 18.

Strausberg, C. (Sep 10, 2002). *9/11 Did Not Stop Police Brutality.* Chicago Defender, p. 1

Tankard, James W., Jr. and Murray C. Harris. (1980). A Discriminant Analysis of Television Viewers and Nonviewers. Journal of Broadcasting, 24(3), 399-409.

U.S. Department of Justice Federal Bureau of Investigation. 2004. Terrorism 2000/2001. www.fbi.gov/publications/terror/terror2000_2001.htm [accessed 5/10/06]

Tuchman, Gaye (1978). Making news: a study in the construction of reality. New York: The Free Press.

U.S. Department of State. Significant terrorist incidents, 1961-2003: a brief chronology. http://www.state.gov/r/pa/ho/pubs/fs/5902.htm

Van Dijk, E., & Wilke, H. (1997). Is this mine or is it ours? Framing property rights and decision making in social dilemmas. Organizational Behavior and Human Decision Processes, 71, 195–209.

Van Dijk, T. A. (1988). News as discourse. Hillsdale, NJ: Lawrence Erlbaum Associates, Inc.

Watkins, C. (2001). Framing protest: news media frames of the Million Man March. Critical Studies in Media Communication. 18 (1) 83-101.

Weaver, D., Drrew, D., & Wilhoit, G. C. (1985). A profile of U.S. radio and television journalist. Paper presented at the Radio Television Division at the annual meeting of the Association for Education in Journalism and Mass Communication, Memphis, TN.

Wells, M. (2005). Random searches divide New York. Story from BBC NEWS: http://news.bbc.co.uk/go/pr/fr/-/2/hi/americas/4747463.stm, New York [accessed 5/09/05].

White, D. M. (1950). The "Gatekeeper": A Case Study in the Selection of News. Journalism Quarterly 27(4): 383-390.

Whitney, D. C. & Becker, L. B. (1982). Keeping the gates for gatekeepers: the effects of wire news. Journalism Quarterly, 59, 60-65.

Willis, A. (2003). The Roots of Racial Profiling. Notes and Documents of Free Persons of Color: Colonial Virginia, 1650-1850

Wilson, C. C., II, & Gutierrez, F. (1995). Race, multiculturalism, and the media. Thousand Oaks, CA: Sage.

Wilson, K. (Jun 9, 2000). *Group says U.S. waging drug war against Blacks.* Philadelphia Tribune, p. 5.

Wolseley, R.E. (1990). The Black Press U.S.A. (2nd ed.). Ames, IA.:

Yohnka, E. (2006). Legislative Panel Urged to Make Permanent, Expand Steps to Confront Racial Profiling in Illinois. U.S. Newswire.

Zaller, J. R. (1992). The nature and origins of mass opinion. New York: Cambridge University Press. The Road to War: Breaking the Code 8

Zogby International accessed 11-8-01 http://www.zogby.com/soundbites/ReadClips.dbm?ID=3965

Vita

Mia Moody, Ph.D., is a professor of journalism at Baylor University. Her teaching and research interests include minorities in the media, coverage of presidential campaigns, and frame analysis of various issues. Moody is editor of the *Missionary Baptist General Convention of Texas ' Women's Ministry Magazine*, and a blogger for the *Waco Tribune-Herald*. Previously, she was editor and publisher of *"FOR" Seasons* and *Elegant Woman* magazines.